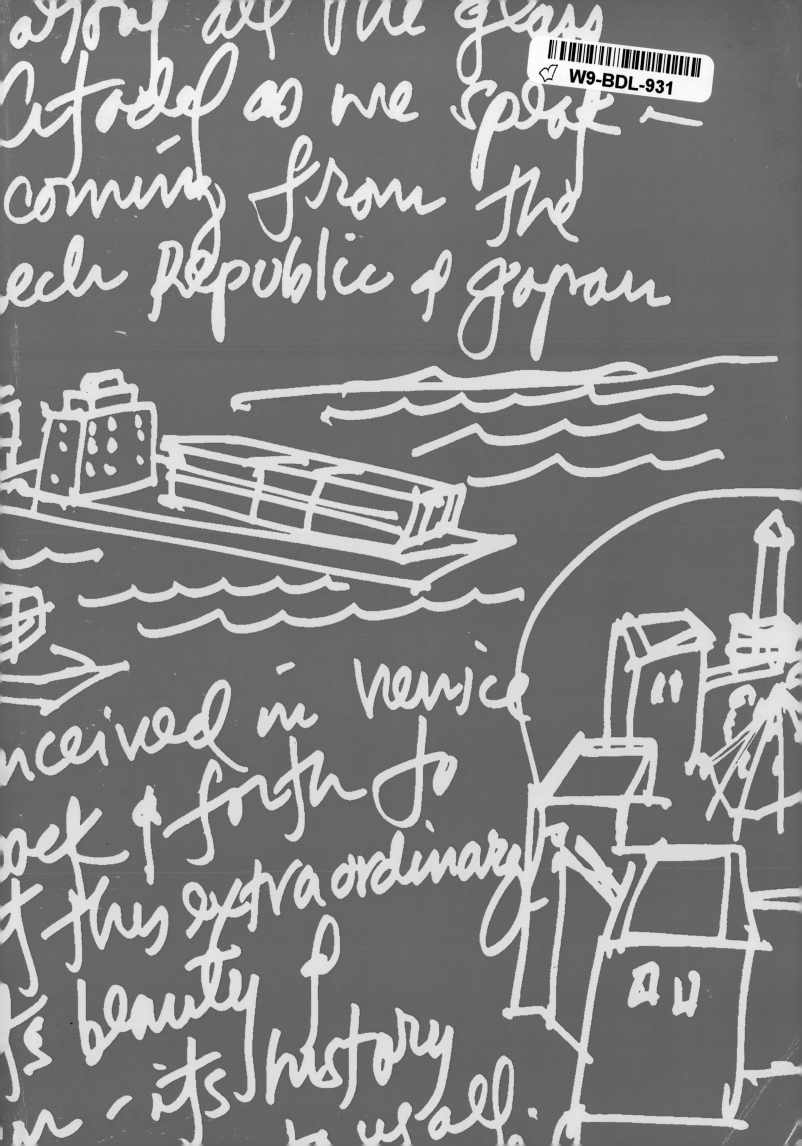

Tower of David
Museum of the History of Jerusalem

צ'יהולי
ירושלים 2000

CHIHULY JERUSALEM 2000

تشيهولي
اورشليم القدس ٢٠٠٠

† PORTLAND PRESS

For Jerusalem
and the memory of
Izzika Gaon

The Tower of David and Chihuly's Glass Exhibition

Jerusalem holds a unique place in the consciousness of the Western world. It is not only central to the three major monotheistic religions but also the present day embodiment of rich ancient civilizations, which have helped to define the nature of the country today. The archaeology of the city continues to uncover the manifold splendors of the past.

At the center of Jerusalem, at the Jaffa Gate entrance to Jerusalem's Old City, stands the Tower of David, the seven-hundred-year-old restored Citadel. It stands between East and West, and between old and new, at the edge of four thousand years of history and the modern city that began to flourish in the mid-nineteenth century. The Citadel is an identifiable element of the city's skyline even for those who do not know what lies inside its thick, fortified walls. Today, the Citadel houses a museum of the history of Jerusalem, a unique institution that recounts four thousand years of Jerusalem's history in a manner that makes this remarkable story easily comprehensible to visitors from diverse backgrounds and countries. There is a balanced presentation focusing on the significance of the city as a site revered throughout its long and turbulent past by three major religions.

The location of the museum plays an important role. The very stones in the Citadel courtyard represent a microcosm of the history of the city, the history that the museum recounts in detail, thereby creating a symbiotic relationship between the archaeological elements outside the museum and the flow of the exhibition within its walls.

There is evidence that man made beads in glass as early as four thousand years ago. The Canaanites, who lived in what is now modern day Israel during the 14th–13th centuries B.C., practiced this art form. But glass as material was incidental to the form created, and often the glass was made to look like marble, then more highly prized than glass.

It was in the Mediterranean at the start of the first millennium, two thousand years ago, that man discovered how to blow glass and create forms which are natural to the medium of glass, allowing the material to find full expression. A direct line from these works of art in glass can be traced to the artistic creations of Dale Chihuly at the end of the second millennium.

During Chihuly's short visit to Jerusalem in 1997, he was immediately struck by the Citadel as a perfect location for his glass installations. Chihuly's exhibition at the Citadel has altered the skyline of Jerusalem. His magnificent installations in glass are making their mark in the next chapter of the city's rich history, filling the Citadel with light and color.

In retrospect, Chihuly's encounter with Jerusalem seems inevitable, and the mounting of his dramatic installations over the city is a most fitting celebration of the millennium.

Shosh Yaniv, Director
Tower of David • Museum of the History of Jerusalem

the Tower of David
Museum of the History of Jerusalem

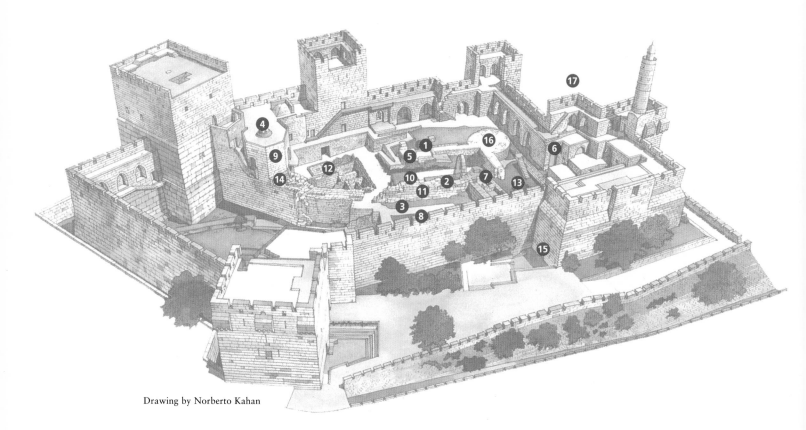

Drawing by Norberto Kahan

Contents

The following is Chihuly's fax to his son, Jackson, ("Mighty")
dated April 22, 1999. As it turns out, certain installations were
scrapped and others were added, but in general, the project
turned out to be close to Chihuly's fax.

mighty meth have got mountain climbers from Israel or elsewhere to scale the Citadel walls both outside & inside to put flowers — thousands of them — coming out of everywhere — Imagine nights with the sun coming through them!

18

MOON BALL is the name of

this my (Mighty) - sorry about
my writing - it's bumpy
on this Tokyo - San Fran.
run on april 26 - 1999.
I just went to my
show in Hiroshima
another city like
Jerusalem that
had to be rebuilt
many times from
the scars of war.
The Moon Ball
is going to be
blue/green colors
something like
the Atlantis
piece.

YELLOW FISH: they've been called

CHIHULY STUDIO 509 NE NORTHLAKE WAY SEATTLE, WA 98105
TEL: 206 632 8707 FAX: 206-632-8825

These too were made in France. There's only about 25 of them & they're in a beautiful uranium yellow color. Hope you don't get bored with all this glass (highrise) but they'll be all kinds of team members that will want to play with you & lots of visitors & friends that are coming

might the glass blower like to name the forms sometimes while they're blowing them

they call these

they'll be a

the

BLUE HERONS

couple hundred of these herons — maybe coming out of one

of the tower

some of them are Black

BLACK 4 RED SEGUAROS (sp?) they look
a little like those big cacti from Sonoran
Desert in Arizona (mighty). They'll feel right
at home in the nearby desert of Israel.
We'll put them on top one of the towers.

I think we have a couple of hundred of them.

They were made in Finland.

CHIHULY STUDIO 509 NE NORTHLAKE WAY SEATTLE, WA 98105
TEL: 206 632 8707 FAX 206 632 8932

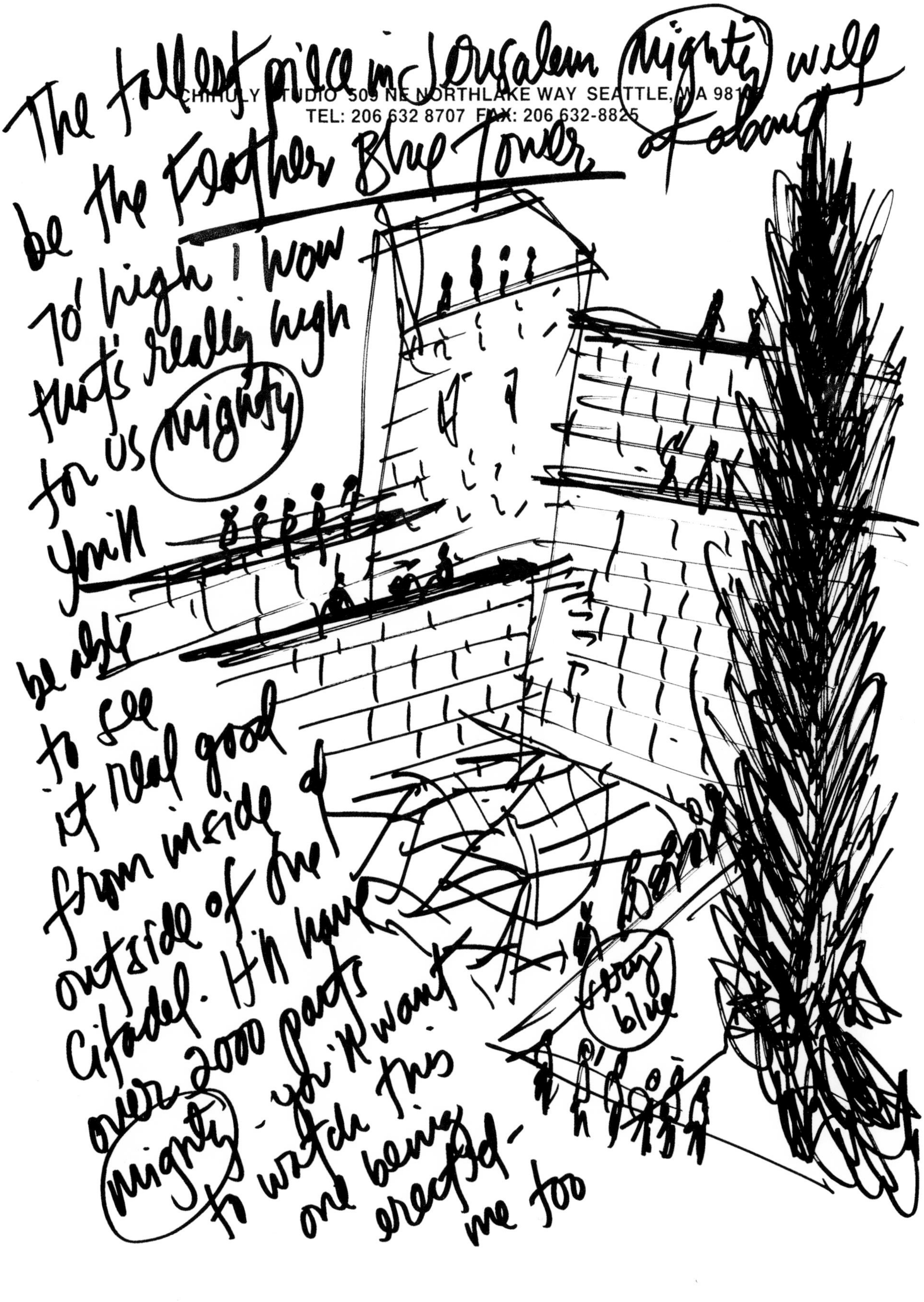

The tallest piece in Jerusalem (mighty) will be the Feather Blue Tower _about

70' high! wow that's really high for us (mighty) You'll be able to see it real good from inside of outside of the Citadel. It'll have over 2000 parts (mighty) - you'll want this to watch this one being erected - me too

feather

sooty blue

"Mighty" I call them. SPEARS & they can be as long
as 20 feet the longest forms I've ever blown - US Vally
like them in red & orange but not always we'll have
about 500 SPEAR in Jerusalem

I think Mighty is the SPEAR FOREST somewhere?

CHIHULY STUDIO 509 NE NORTHLAKE WAY SEATTLE, WA 98105
TEL: 206 632 9107 FAX: 206 632-8825

Moon
Ball — w
curly
1.22.99.

Floats in the ancient village

37000' en route Tokyo
4.22.99.

Reprinted with permission from **Ariel:**
The Israel Review of Arts and Letters,
Vol. 111, 1999, by Dale Chihuly

Chihuly in the Light of Jerusalem 2000

There are many reasons why I came to Jerusalem and the Tower of David Museum to make a major exhibition. First there was my stay at Kibbutz Lahav in 1962–63. I remember arriving at the kibbutz as a boy of 21 and leaving a man, just a few short months later. Before Lahav my life was more about having fun, and after Lahav I wanted to make some sort of contribution to society—I discovered there was more to life than having a good time. It's difficult to explain how this change came about, but it had a lot to do with going out on border patrol during the night with guys my own age who had more responsibility and maturity than adults twice their age in the States. After the Kibbutz experience my life would never be the same.

The best and most famous book about Venice is by Ruskin, called the "Stones of Venice." All of Venice is stone with the exception of the canals, which are lined with stone. I think it's for this reason that Jerusalem, which is also built entirely of stone, reminds me so much of Venice. And they are both such historic cities—especially the Old City of Jerusalem, which has changed so very little over the centuries. Both Venice and Jerusalem allow you to experience them as if you were in a previous century. Both are such beautiful, magical places with a very special quality of light and atmosphere. Two of the most unique cities in the world that are both beyond comparison and without envy.

Another exciting and thrilling component of "Chihuly in the Light of Jerusalem 2000" is the Holy Land, where glass was invented some 4,000 years ago, somewhere along the shores of the Mediterranean. Legend has it that there was a shipwreck, and the sailors who got to the beach built a bonfire and used some blocks of soda that had been part of the cargo for seating around the fire. During the night a block of soda fell into the fire, which acted like a flux, which lowers the melting point of sand. When they woke in the morning they discovered they had made a batch of glass. Whether or not this story is true, archaeologists are certain this is the area where glass was invented, undoubtedly by accident, and the people who did it were bright enough to realize the importance of their discovery.

Not only was glass discovered here, but some 2,000 years later, just before the birth of Christ, glassblowing was invented, probably by accident as well. This extraordinary discovery turned out to be even more important than the invention of glass itself. Now there was a way to make inexpensive containers that would hold liquid, not be porous, never leak, and in which one could see the contents. An extremely functional and beautiful vessel that immediately became highly sought after. The craft of glassblowing quickly spread throughout the area, and because of its immediate widespread success it is difficult to pinpoint its exact point of invention. One can only wonder what kind of genius thought of blowing human breath down a metal tube, forming a bubble inside a molten blob of glass.

And to think that this molten blob of glass is made only of silica or sand, the most common material in the world, that can be transformed from a solid to a liquid to a solid from just fire. For me it's the most mysterious and magical of all the inventions or materials that mankind has invented or discovered. Since I was a little boy I always loved glass. And 34 years ago I put a pipe into some stained glass that melted in my basement, and blew a bubble. Since that moment I have spent my life as an explorer searching for new ways to use glass and glassblowing to make forms and colours and installations that no one has ever created before—that's what I love to do. The Jerusalem project started with a lunch on my kitchen table about two years ago with Izzika and Yaffa Gaon. [Izzika Gaon, who died in 1997, was Chief Curator of Design at the Israel Museum, Jerusalem.] They had visited Venice when I hung chandeliers over the canals and we all thought a special installation project would be great for Israel, and the Citadel of David came up as an extraordinary location for such a project. When Izzika died shortly after, I flew to Jerusalem for his memorial service and met Shosh Yaniv, the Museum director, and she gave me a tour of the Citadel. I was totally overwhelmed with the Citadel and Jerusalem, which I had visited once before in 1962. Shosh and I were determined to find a way to do this project in Izzika's memory.

Initially we set the budget at 250,000 dollars and I thought I might build three towers in the courtyard of the Citadel in honour of the three main religions in Jerusalem. I visited Jerusalem and the Citadel two more times before the project and with each trip I tried to increase the size and scope of the project. It ended up with four installations and a retrospective exhibition in the Crusader's Hall.

In the end "Chihuly in the Light of Jerusalem 2000" cost over one million dollars. Of course, as the budget size and number of installations increased so did the need for a larger installation team and support group. We also felt that we could no longer fabricate in

Seattle all of the intricate and complicated armatures of steel that would be needed for the Crystal Mountain, the Blue Tower, the Moon and the Persian Seaform Ceiling. Our site engineer would go to Jerusalem to work for two months prior to the installation team in order to design and erect the structure. We then planned on the team to have three weeks to build the installations. In addition to the 30 people from the Boathouse [Chihuly's home workshop in Seattle], we felt we would need an additional 30–40 Israelis to help us mount the installations and a large crane to move some of the structures into place. In the end our calculations turned out perfectly, and we finished the Crystal Mountain the day before the opening on July 1, 1999.

Many people have asked me what was I thinking and why—how did I go about creating the pieces—do they have a meaning? I guess the answer is that I think from my gut more than my head. I walked around the Citadel many times, trying to get a feeling for the architecture—understanding the space or the "room" that developed over the centuries. The colour of the stone, the ground, the sky. What felt right for the space? How many pieces? What colour and what form? I knew that Jews, Moslems, Christians and tourists from around the world would visit—as many as a million people would now see the Citadel in an altered way. I wanted my work to enhance their visit to the Citadel. Some pieces would be obvious and others would be discovered. Some very colourful and others subtle. Some going upwards and others down into the excavations. Some very beautiful and others more unusual and raw. Colours and form are seen first, and I wanted to have a variety of colours but not have it feel like

I picked one of each colour, so I used white, pink and blue for the major pieces in addition to the red and yellow spears. After these pieces were installed we placed the smaller groups, many of which had brighter colours. One of the most exciting things about the Citadel was the many vantage points from which to view the exhibition. You could see the installations from every level and almost every angle, which is totally different than the experience one has in a museum where the viewpoints are controlled.

The most complicated piece in the exhibition is the Crystal Mountain. It was a new idea for me in almost every way, and it was built for the first time in the Citadel. The steel structure for the mountain weighs over 34,000 kilograms and has 18,000 welds and nearly five kilometers of metal building rods. It was engineered and took about six weeks to fabricate on location in the Citadel. We then added 2,000 polyvitro crystals to the end points of the rods which weighed over 1,000 kilos. It turned out nearly 15 metres high and over 11 metres in diameter, built on top of an ancient Islamic tower base. I chose a gold pink colour for the crystals because it is bright and light and joyous on top of the heavy steel structure. This piece, more than any of the installations, was made for the Jerusalem sun and light and works at its best at sunrise and sunset.

Most of my installations in the past were designed for museums and indoor applications and rely primarily on artificial lighting. And although we did ship and install some 200 lighting fixtures for night viewing, the primary viewing in the Citadel is of course during daylight hours. The sun is much brighter than any artificial sources so the colours seem much different. Certain colours look fantastic in the bright sun—the Red and Yellow Spears, the Blue Tower, the Silver Star and the Saguaros. I chose pieces that would take the strong light and many colours won't. In the end the installations came from five countries: the US, France, Finland, Japan and the Czech Republic. We also created a small installation of local Hebron glass made in the ancient tradition.

So here we are, some two years later, watching the dream unfold. It is a tribute to Izzika Gaon, but in the broader sense it is a tribute to 4000 years of glass making here in the Holy Land—and even more important—a tribute to a unique site in a unique city in a unique country and at a unique time. As we stand on the threshold of the new millennium here at the ancient Tower of David, this is my own personal tribute—Chihuly in the Light of Jerusalem 2000.

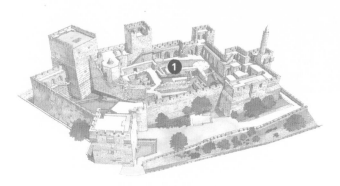

Red Spears · Finland and France

"I thought Venice was the ultimate city, but the stone
and the history of Jerusalem, its complexity, make
this an even more fascinating place. It couldn't be
more beautiful. The juxtaposition of stone, one
of the hardest materials that has stood the test of
time, and glass, the most fragile, transparent material,
gave me another reason to work in this great city."

Dale Chihuly, Hadassah Magazine,
December 1999

"And so, we continue to visit these factories around the world because we enjoy working with craftsmen and artisans; glass is different, equipment is different, and the colors are different. It's very challenging, and you'll never know what new forms will come from it."

Dale Chihuly, lecture at Rackham Auditorium,
University of Michigan, Ann Arbor, November 2, 1999

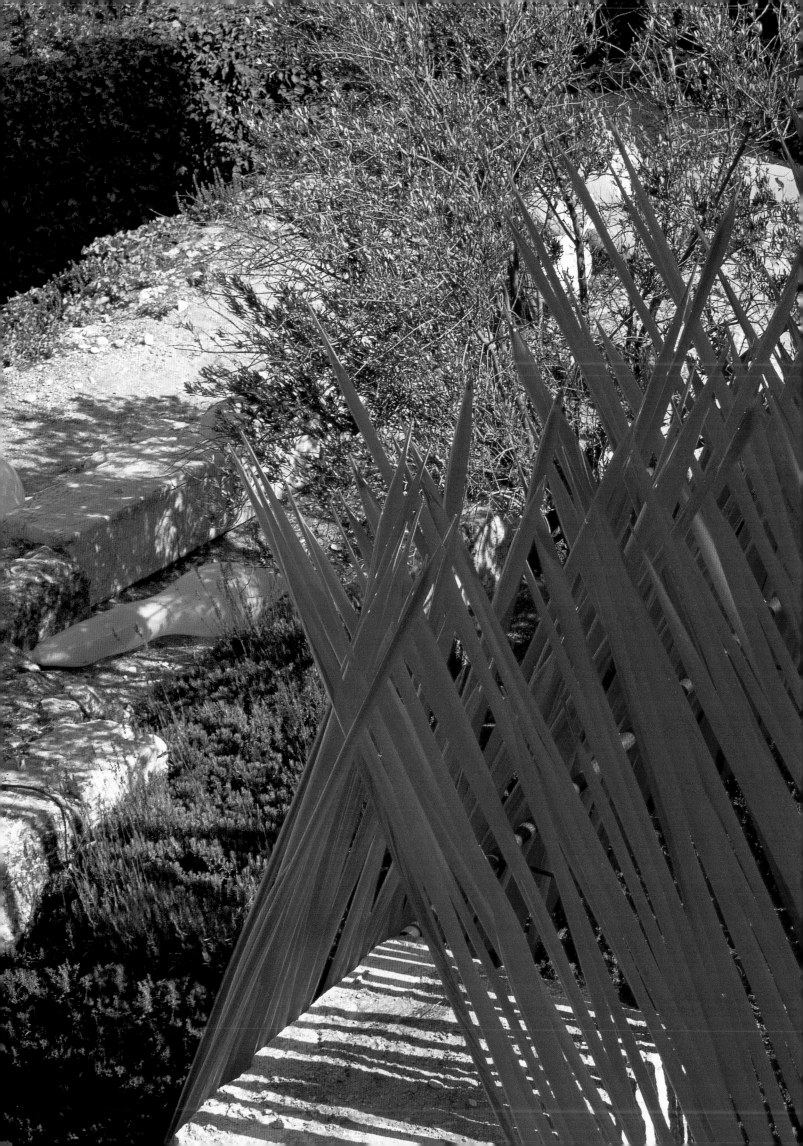

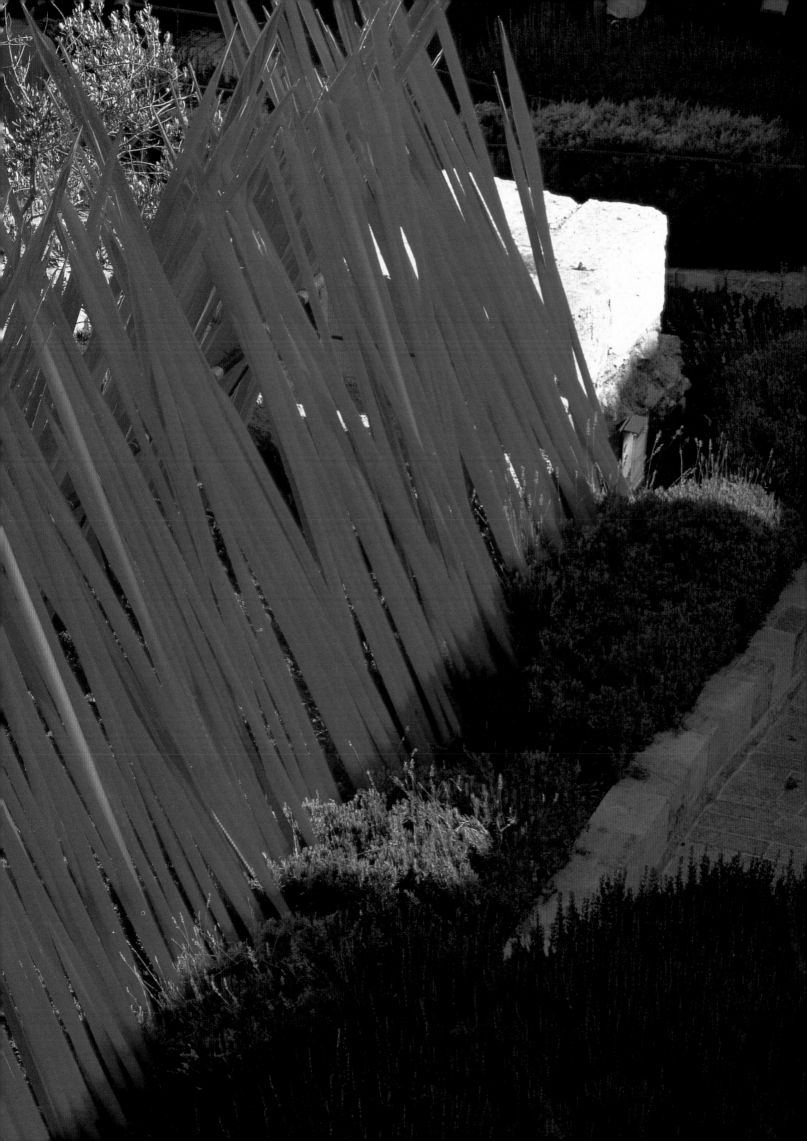

White Tower · Czech Republic

"At first, the modern art seems out of place, but
then the contrast of old and new begins to fit together.
A mountain of glass fits right over the base of an
ancient watchtower. A glass tree is highlighted by a
Crusader arch. Green leaves of glass are just the
right ornaments along the pathways. And huge
balls of blue glass resting at the bottom of the water
cisterns may have been there for centuries."

www.about.com, accessed July 19, 1999,
"Chihuly at the Tower of David," by Ellis Shuman

"I work with four materials: glass, plastic, ice and water. These are the only materials of any scale that are transparent. When you look at their transparency, what you are looking at is light itself—with all the rest of the hundred thousand materials you are seeing reflected light. Transmitted light is infinitely more powerful, more mysterious and beautiful. That's why glass, ice, water and plastic have always fascinated people."

Dale Chihuly, 1999

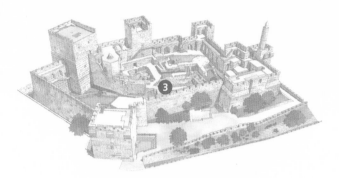

Green Grass · Czech Republic

"Here was a piece that didn't work. I made the spikes in the Czech Republic. They were green, uranium green. I wanted this beautiful green, which you can't get in this country because of the oxide it takes to make it. Anyway, I get them, but they're just too stiff for me. So I hung them as a chandelier. It was kind of a nice chandelier, but it still didn't work. It was just too spiky. Maybe on a different day I could have made it work. But, at that time and that place, it just wasn't meant to be. So I said, take it down and make some green grass."

Dale Chihuly, lecture at Glendale Foothills Public Library, Glendale, Arizona, November 21, 1999

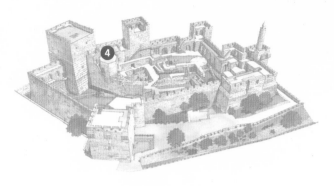

Moon · USA

"34 years ago I put a pipe into some stained glass that I melted in my basement, and blew a bubble. Since that moment I have spent my life as an explorer searching for new ways to use glass and glassblowing to make forms and colours and installations that no one has ever created before me—that's what I love to do."

Ariel: The Israel Review of Arts and Letters, Vol. 111, 1999, by Dale Chihuly

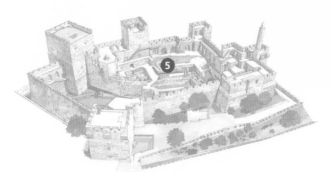

White Seal Pups · France

"In many ways Jerusalem was a very spiritual experience for me. Each time I returned to the Citadel, I got more involved and the project got bigger and bigger as I became more connected to Jerusalem. There's something very special about Jerusalem. I can't tell you exactly what it is, but there's no place on earth quite like it."

Dale Chihuly, lecture at California Center for the Arts, Escondido, California, November 15, 1999

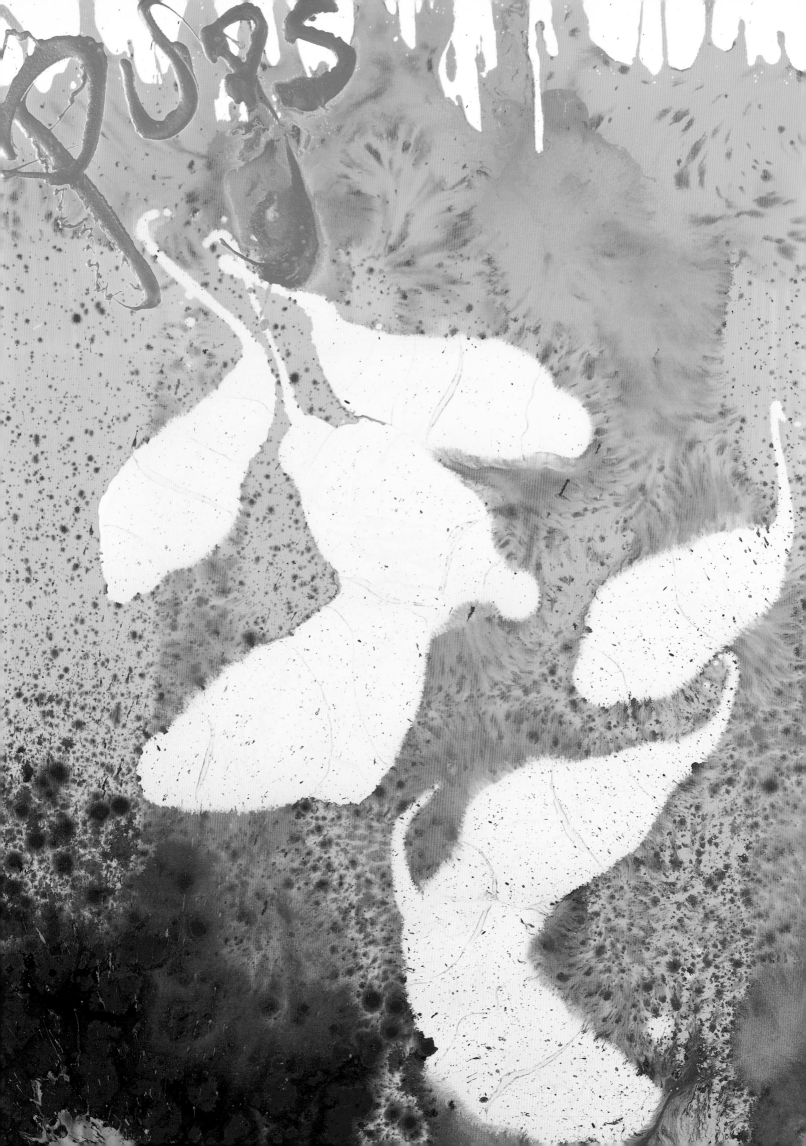

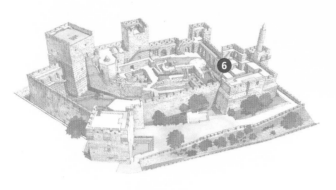

Star · USA

"Two of the pieces in the exhibition are made of plastic and the rest are glass. Plastic and glass are the only materials that you would silver or mirror on the inside. I am not sure when mirroring was invented, but it's a magical process that allows light to go through the plastic and glass and then bounce right back to you with the same intensity. Try to imagine a world without mirrors. What a great invention that we take for granted."

Dale Chihuly, lecture at Victoria and Albert Museum,
London, October 13, 1999

"Originally the pieces that make up the Star chandelier were meant to go on the outside walls of the Citadel. I made them out of plastic so they were lightweight and couldn't be vandalized. I brought over a couple of mountain climbers to secure the plastic parts onto the fifty-foot-high walls of the Citadel, but we couldn't figure out a way to attach the pieces to the walls without damaging the stones, so we stopped and made them into the Star chandelier. The light-weight parts allow me to build pieces that weigh a lot less, and sometimes that's essential."

Dale Chihuly, lecture at Victoria and Albert Museum, London, October 13, 1999

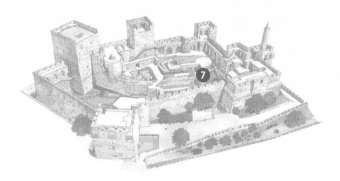

Red Saguaros · Finland

"The Red Saguaros were made in Finland from a beautiful ruby red glass. It's a very difficult red formula to melt, and that's one of the reasons I like to work in Finland. All of the different red, yellow, orange, and ambers you see in this sculpture are the same batch of ruby red. Only glass has this ability to make so many variations from the same exact composition. It's like a gift from the gods."

Dale Chihuly, lecture at Glendale Foothills Public Library, Glendale, Arizona, November 21, 1999

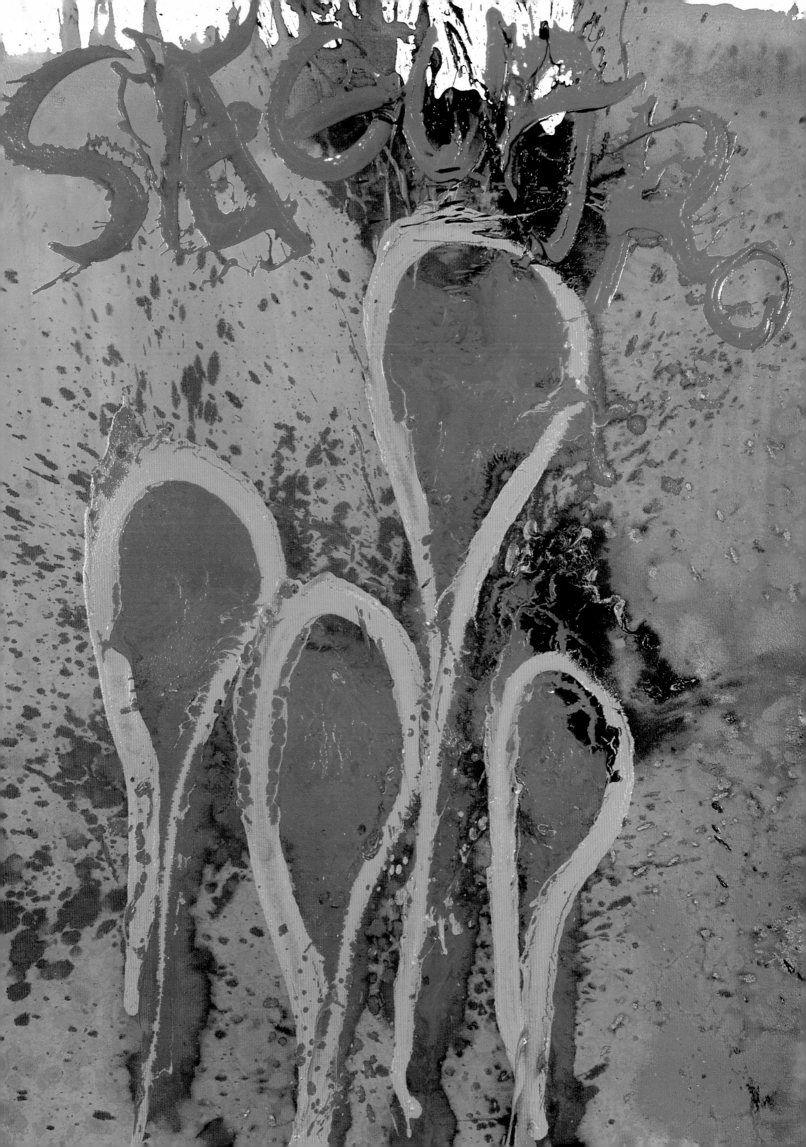

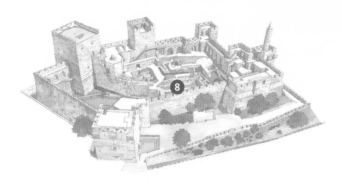

Blue Tower · USA

"At one point I was going to make three towers—
one for Judaism, one for Christianity, and one for
Islam—but in the end I decided not to do that.
Obviously people are going to look at them and see
things they want to see in them. I prefer that than if
I told them what it is that they should be seeing."

St. Louis Jewish Light, October 13, 1999,
"Artist Transforms Part of Jerusalem into City of Glass,"
by Avi Machlis

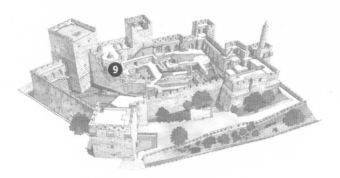

Yellow Chandelier · USA

"And I use my drawings, whatever it takes for me
to communicate, with the glassblowers, with the
installers, or the architects or engineers that I work
with. Whatever it takes to communicate is what I do.
And the way I communicate, with different artists,
it's different for everybody; there is no set way that I
do things. Sometimes it's talking in person, sometimes it's working with drawings, sometimes it's
looking at photographs. Whatever it takes to get
where I want to get to is what I try to do. And I find
that everybody that I work with is different. So it
takes different ways to try to explain what I want to
have happen."

Dale Chihuly, lecture at Victoria and Albert Museum,
London, October 13, 1999

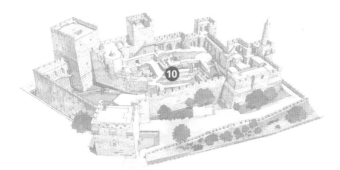

Fishing Floats · Japan

"When I was working blowing glass in Japan a few years ago, I started making large floats, those big colored balls. But I also heard about this Japanese glassblower—the last one to make the real fishing floats. So I found out that he lived up in Hokkaido, he was seventy-eight years old, and we went up and visited him. Then I ordered one thousand fishing floats from him. I had no idea what the hell I was going to do with them, so they sat around, one thousand, mostly still in boxes, sat around my studio for a couple of years. I decided to take them to Israel and put them down into one of these pits, one of these digs."

Dale Chihuly, lecture at Victoria and Albert Museum, London, October 13, 1999

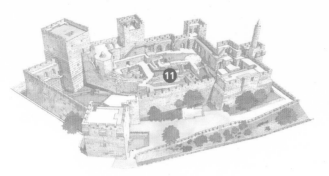

Black Saguaros · Finland

"I work on things over and over. If you were to come
to my studio, you would see a big team of people
working, usually making the same thing all day. So
it would be the same thing, over and over and over
and over. And in that way, you begin to be able
to control what's going on. We are using gravity,
centrifugal force, the heat, the fire, all of these different elements, and in many ways we are not totally
in control. It's letting the glass also make the form.
Going with it, I want the pieces to be very often as
if they are from nature. And so you are not sure, is
it man-made? Is it made by nature?"

Dale Chihuly, lecture at Victoria and Albert Museum,
London, October 13, 1999

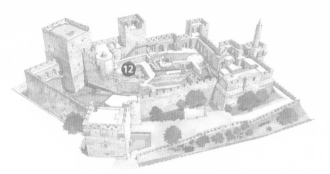

Niijima Floats · USA

"This is the first piece you see when you come in. You're looking down about thirty or forty feet into this old village. I don't remember how old it is, at least a couple of thousand years old, that's been excavated. There's not much in there for scale but those floats; the biggest ones are about three feet in diameter."

Dale Chihuly, lecture at Rackham Auditorium,
University of Michigan, Ann Arbor, November 2, 1999

"Usually we can control the museum shows, the lighting, a little bit like the way you can control a stage set. You can do a lot on the stage that people aren't aware of to make things look a certain way. It's the same way in a museum show, because I design the museum show, and very often pieces are seen from only one vantage point, and I can light it really beautifully. I can control the amount of ambient light. This was different. This was shown at night and in broad daylight, with this incredible desert sun."

Dale Chihuly, lecture at Rackham Auditorium,
University of Michigan, Ann Arbor, November 2, 1999

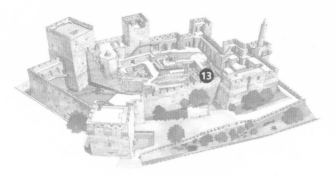

Yellow Spears · France

"Many people have asked me what I was thinking and why—how did I go about creating the pieces—do they have a meaning? I guess the answer is that I think from my gut more than my head. I walked around the Citadel many times, trying to get a feeling for the architecture—understanding the space or the "room" that developed over the centuries. The colour of the stone, the ground, the sky. What felt right for the space? How many pieces? What colour and what form? . . . Some pieces would be obvious and others would be discovered. Some very colourful and others subtle. Some going upwards and others down into the excavations. Some very beautiful and others more unusual and raw."

Ariel: The Israel Review of Arts and Letters, Vol. 111, 1999, by Dale Chihuly

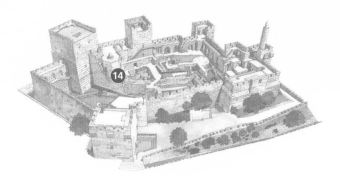

Hebron Vessels · Israel

"I went over to Hebron, the Arab village ten or twenty miles from Jerusalem, where there is a tradition of glassblowing. They still blow glass the same way they did five hundred years ago. They work on their laps, not with a glassblowing bench, but right on their legs, working by themselves. And so I went to visit the Hebron glassblowers. I looked at what they made. Again, I really didn't alter what they made, just a little bit, and had them make me a couple of hundred pieces so we could do an Arab installation in the Citadel as well."

Dale Chihuly, lecture at California Center for the Arts, Escondido, California, November 15, 1999

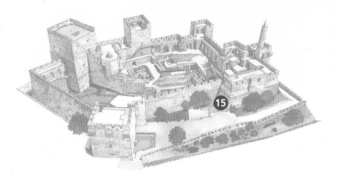

Jerusalem Cylinders · USA

"I've always wanted to do a series of blown objects with chunks of crystals on them—I love the look of glass crystals. The challenge was how to make the crystals and then how to apply them to the cylinders and be able to reheat them without the crystals losing their beautiful sharp edges."

Dale Chihuly, from a fax to his son, "Mighty," June 13, 1999

JUNE 13 · 1999

CHIHULY STUDIO 1111 NW 50TH STREET SEATTLE, WA 98107-5120
TEL: 206 781 8707 FAX: 206 781-1906

I know that you loved watching the cylinders — not all of them are cylinders. I made some cone shapes like the crystal mountain. It's great stuff that you like the glassblowing & that you're not afraid of the furnaces (you don't seem to be afraid of anything). It won't be long & you'll be blowing glass might & we'll see if you like it? I got a feeling you will. Enjoy this little book on the JERUSALEM CYLINDERS & THE CRYSTAL MOUNTAINS — I love 'em & I'm very proud of them & the great crew that made them.

your
Dad —

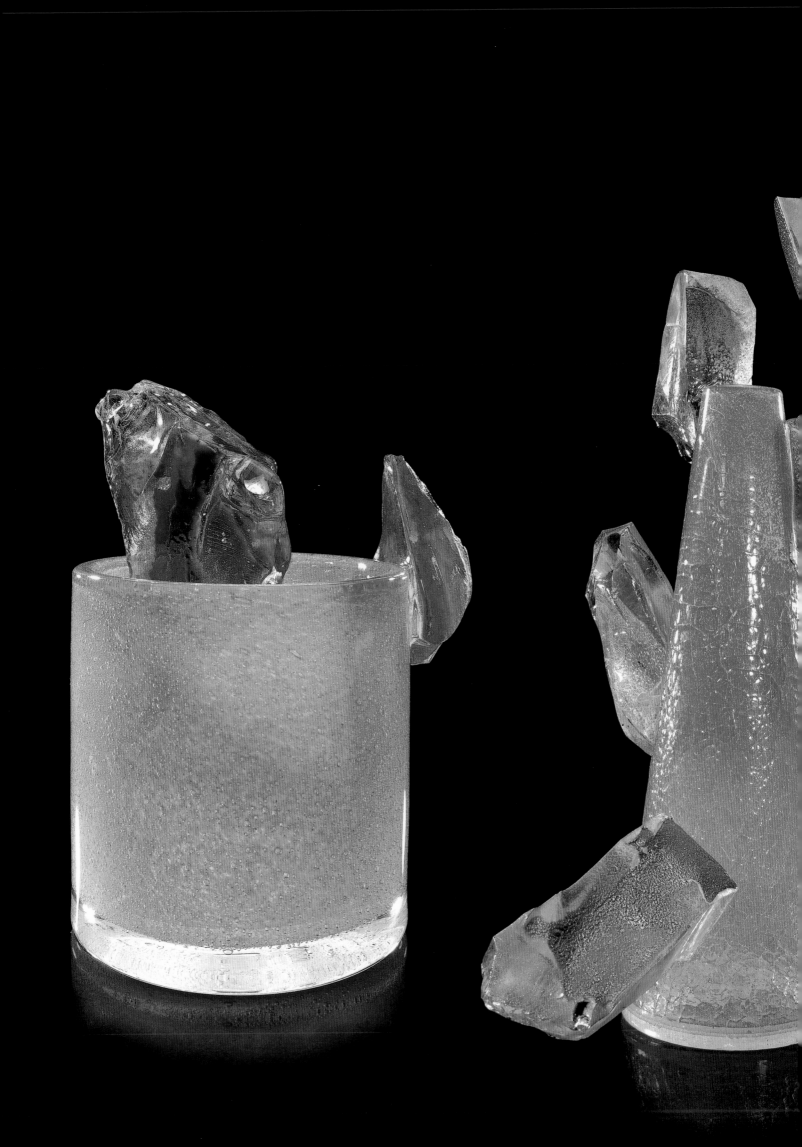

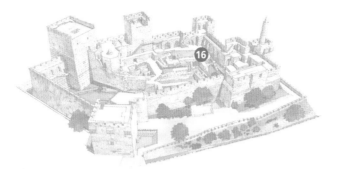

Crystal Mountain · USA

"There are sides to the Crystal Mountain that aren't so pretty, sort of "brutto," you know, because it reveals its inner structure so much: the steel and the five kilometers of reinforcing rod, eighteen thousand welds, big high beams. The structure is a very important part of it, and of course the more crystals we put on it, the more we covered the structure. If we wanted to we could cover it entirely, but then the sunlight wouldn't penetrate from one side to the other, so we left it fairly open."

Dale Chihuly, "Chihuly in the Light of Jerusalem 2000,"
Video by Peter West, Portland Press 1999

Jerusalem 2000

"What am I going to do in here where the scale would work with the Citadel? I don't want to make it too big. I don't want to make it too small. So I decided I would make the Crystal Mountain, and I was going to make it out of glass. I started mining glass out of old factories, where I could go in with a jackhammer and get big chunks of crystal. We found they were hard to work with. They weren't stable enough, and I decided, eventually, to take molds off of those crystals and then cast them in plastic. . . Don't ask me why I picked pink, but I did."

Dale Chihuly, lecture at Rackham Auditorium,
University of Michigan, Ann Arbor, November 2, 1999

Jerusalem Wall of Ice · Israel

"When I was a young man, I went to Alaska as a commercial fisherman on a salmon trawler. Twenty years later I did a series of exhibitions in Alaska. I was then shown a snapshot of a three-ton block of ice . . . that was on a forklift being lifted out of the ice fields near Fairbanks. At that moment I thought of taking the ice blocks to Israel. The idea of taking these huge blocks of crystal from Alaska to Israel, halfway around the world, was a dream, an idea, but I didn't forget it. So when I did 'Chihuly in the Light of Jerusalem 2000' in the Tower of David Museum in the Old City, I thought once again about the ice from Alaska. I wanted to give something back to the Jerusalemites for accepting my work in such a heartfelt way. So I brought them sixty-four tons of Alaska ice in the form of twenty-four blocks —known as 'Arctic Diamonds.'"

The Republic, October 11, 1999,
"Crystal Mountain Dream Come True," by Dale Chihuly

"But the quality of the ice was really something. In the way that you could see through it some of the time, it would get hazy some of the time, it would crackle, it would make noise, it would fissure, there were things going on, it was alive, this ice."

Dale Chihuly, lecture at Victoria and Albert Museum, London, October 13, 1999

Reprinted with permission from
The Art Newspaper, International Edition,
May 1999, by Sarah Greenberg

Glass Act

Setting off to see Dale Chihuly is a bit like searching for the Wizard of Oz. The celebrity glass artist resides in Seattle, the nearest thing to the Emerald City that America can offer, and, like the famous wizard, he dwells in a colourful world of his own making—one in which he changes his mind from a moment to the next and his entranced team of assistants hurries to keep pace.

The day our interview had been scheduled and a flight to Seattle booked, he decided the weather was too cold and jetted down to his desert home in Palm Springs. "This happens all the time. His plans change daily, even hourly. There are 150 people working here. Our sole purpose is to keep up with him and we cannot keep up," explains his chief assistant, Joanna Sikes. "After you've spent a few days seeing everything here just fly down to the desert and visit him there," she suggested, as I arrived for what was supposed to be an afternoon appointment at the Boathouse: the "hot shop," headquarters and home of the master of glass, whom people around here refer to as "the rock star."

Glass art's answer to Nirvana has a lot to answer for.

For one thing, he has pulled glass off the shelf and into the world. Whether one calls them garish or glorious—or both—Chihuly's fantastical glass forms are growing bigger all the time and they are multiplying. From the Bellagio Casino in Las Vegas to the new line of Disney Cruise ships, the Paradise Island resort in the Bahamas and the Rainbow Room in Rockefeller Center to the American embassies in London, Paris and Dublin, Chihuly is spreading. In 1995–96 he embarked on one of the largest art projects ever undertaken: leading his team of glass-blowers around the world to make and exhibit his trademark chandeliers in four different places famous for their glass—Finland, Ireland, Mexico and Venice. In "Chihuly over Venice," organised to coincide with the first Venezia Vetro Biennale, he placed nineteen quivering glass installations all over the city, from the Doges' Palace to the gondola yard of San Trovaso.

At present he is busy planning his next and biggest project: building a twenty-five-foot mountain of pink glass at the ancient Citadel of David in Jerusalem's Old City to mark the millennium. This autumn, he is breaking ground on the Chihuly Bridge of Glass in his hometown of Tacoma, Washington, which will link the city's new International Glass Museum (scheduled for completion in 2001) with Union Station, a train depot filled with Chihuly's glass installations. This November he has been invited to make a piece for London's Victoria & Albert Museum to emphasise their new commitment to contemporary art. In the year 2000, he is planning "Chihuly over Britain," for which he will bring his team to blow glass at factories in Belfast, Edinburgh and Sunderland, in addition to doing a demonstration at London's Royal College of Art.

In any given month there is at least one Chihuly museum show underway somewhere in the world. And those with a spare half a million dollars can commission a Chihuly for the bottom of their pool, floating as a garden ornament in a pond or hanging as a chandelier. Prices start at around $10,000 for small pieces, rise to $75,000 for more modestly sized installations and stretch to $1 million or so, which the Bellagio ceiling is rumoured to have cost. Chihuly does fifty private commissions a year. "We started making the chandeliers in 1992 and we didn't sell any for three years. Now they're the bulk of our business," says Joanna. Chihuly himself does not know exactly how many pieces he executes per year but he registered 1,600 finished pieces in 1998 and does about 600–800 drawings per year. On the morning I have reached him on his cell-phone in the desert, he is completing a set of ten drawings, calling out orders to his assistants like "don't put it in too logically." His helicopter film crew is whirring overhead (he owns a film company, which records all of his work, as well as a publishing company which distributes all of his books and catalogues) and the call-waiting on his phone constantly cuts in. Demand for Dale is high. I am made to feel lucky.

Still, how can a man who claims that glass is the cheapest material known to man, since it is almost entirely made of sand, ask such high prices? "Why do people pay a lot for a piece of steel bent by Mark de Suvero or Richard Serra? It's not about the price of the material, it's what you do to it," he says. "I made the market. I say what the price is and people pay it. But it took me over ten years before I sold my first piece."

Chihuly became interested in glass as an interior design student in the early 1960s, when he wove it into his tapestries; he blew his first glass bubble in 1965, when he experimented with melting glass on his stove (don't try this at home). He then attended the University of Wisconsin to study art because it had the only glass programme in the country. But he did not have his first museum show until 1971 or his first commercial gallery show until 1977. "I still remember pricing the glass cylinders at $1,000 a piece—higher than had been asked for a craft item before," says Chihuly. Eight sold and he has never looked back.

Since then, Chihuly has created an art form, infrastructure and market for glass where none existed before. In 1968, Chihuly built Seattle's first "hot shop"—the workshop with furnaces and ovens where glass is blown. Today Seattle boasts ninety "hot shops," 3,000 people working in glass and over 300 glassblowers—a total higher than that of the island of Murano, where he found his inspiration.

The Pilchuck Glass School outside of Seattle, which he started as a hippy commune with a $2,000 grant in 1971, has turned into a world famous summer school for glass, attracting the top international glassblowers, training 250 students per year and with an annual operating budget of over $2 million. In the past decade, says Chihuly, the market for glass has really revved up. "All the things you need to make a movement have finally come together: artists, galleries, collectors and museums." He has opened up a new market for collecting among people who did not traditionally collect art and increasingly places his glass creations in non-art environments: baseball stadiums (players for the Yankees and the Mariners collect his work); cars (he redesigned a Jeep for General Motors), forests and ponds.

"Everybody responds to glass as a material.

190

Just think of the way people respond when they walk into a medieval cathedral. And if you had to pick one material to define twentieth-century architecture, it would be glass. It is both accessible and exotic. It is ancient and modern, fragile and strong, mysterious and transparent."

And it is fun. Nothing can prepare the uninitiated visitor for the thrill of walking into Dale's "hot shop," his glass studio housed in a former crew boathouse on the shores of Seattle's Lake Union. The sheer scale of it is breathtaking. One wall is covered floor to ceiling in pigments—colour comes in rods, powder, gravel-like chips to create the different effects. Samples of Chihuly's spun candy glass chandelier forms hang from the walls, like pots in a professional kitchen. On another wall, the "glory holes" of the furnaces burn with an orange glow.

The shop floor is teeming with young men who epitomise the Seattle grunge rock look, wearing wraparound shades to protect them from the heat of the furnaces, ski hats, layers of T shirts, baggy trousers and wrist bands to support their wrists against the weight of the blowpipe—if they weren't blowing glass they'd be snowboarding. Wailing refrains of what the lone female glassblower here describes as "angry white boy music" fill the vast room. Joanna assures me that when Dale is here he listens to the Beatles and opera. He also relaxes in his den, filled with a collection of Picasso pots, Pendleton blankets and Northwest Indian baskets, and he exercises in a lap pool lined in his own flower-like "Persian" glass forms.

Paint covers every available surface in the studio; it is dripped on the floor, on the walls, tables, shoes, his workers' clothes. "He draws on every available surface, including us," says Joanna. Dale has tacked up sketches everywhere as models for his blowers. He communicates his ideas with drawings, squirting tubes of acrylic paint wildly to illustrate a form to his team, streaming on veils of colour and shimmer, using a Pollock-like flick of paint to show a reflection—all in a matter of minutes. When he is out of town he sends up to 150 faxes a day, most covered in a web of intricate scribbles. To an innocent bystander, these look like abstract drawings; to his team they are blueprints.

Since 1976, when he lost one eye in a car accident in the English countryside (on the way to visit the artist Peter Blake), Chihuly has worn a patch over one eye and has no depth perception, so he is no longer able to blow glass himself. Instead he draws two-dimensional, "flattened" visions of what he wants to see and then choreographs his team of ten to fifteen glassblowers in a manic dance of blowing, forming and painting the molten glass at a breakneck pace, since the minute the glass cools it can no longer be worked. The master will coach and cajole, gesticulate wildly and embrace his workers as he watches his vision take shape in their hands. He is utterly engaged in the work and even when he is away calls out his instructions in hundreds of daily voice mail messages. After the studio visit, Joanna leads me out into the glass-strewn gravel driveway and says, "Now I'm taking you to see where it's all put together." A short drive leads us to a sound-stage-like structure where Dale's team builds life-sized "sets" to test the installations. For the Bellagio, they built a mock-up of the casino ceiling; for the Disney cruise ships they built the two-story lobbies. Sound, light and structural crews will do anything from hauling in dirt, if a work is supposed to go on the ground, to creating the reflections of water and the effects of wind. The presentation to the client here is a dress rehearsal for the way the work will look and behave once it is installed *in situ*.

At present they are experimenting with ways to build the Jerusalem mountain, a hollow structure for viewers to walk in and around. Should it be a cone or a pyramid? Should they build it out of glass, or the Polyvitro which Dale prefers, a plastic polymer that looks and acts like glass but is substantially lighter and shatter-proof.

All of this is a far cry from Murano, where Chihuly first learned the art of glassblowing while on a Fulbright scholarship at the Venini glass factory in 1968. "I first applied to go to Finland to study ceramics, but it was a period when Americans were stealing a lot of Scandinavian design ideas and marketing them in the States, so the Finns rejected me," says Chihuly. "Then I decided to apply to do glassblowing, and Venice is the Mecca. I sent slides and letters to 300 companies all over Italy and the only one to reply favourably was Venini, the best glass company in Venice. They said I could come for a few weeks only to watch—not to blow. But they did let me make a model."

Chihuly's real accomplishment was to bring Venetian glassblowing techniques and Venetian glassblowers, such as Lino Tagliapietra, Italo Scango and Pino Signoretti, to America, transforming what had been the tiny studio glass movement. As a day-job, he began teaching at the Rhode Island School of Design, where he set up the glass department. In 1971, he gathered a bunch of like-minded people together and started what is perhaps best described as a glassblowing summer love-in at Pilchuck, a tree farm outside Seattle. Tuition was free but students had to bring their own camping gear and food.

"We were part of the Woodstock generation and that whole hippy thing. We wanted to get back to nature. I didn't think we were doing it for anything more than a summer," said Chihuly. The first year they blew glass at a makeshift "hot shop" under a tent in the woods. For ten weeks they tripped-out on glass, experimenting with it in every possible way, from cooking pancakes on hot glass, to floating glass bubbles in the duck pond. "I spent my $2000 teacher's grant and was $7000 in hock," recalls Chihuly. "Then John and Ann Hauberg, who owned the tree farm, donated the land and gave me $20,000 to keep going."

The amazing thing about Pilchuck Glass School today is that despite its world-class status, it still looks like a summer camp. The wood cabins and tree-houses, the tipi-style "hot shop" and laid-back attitude all belie the fact that the school now attracts around 800 applicants for the 250 spots it offers in its series of intense two-week summer school courses. Everybody who is anybody in the glass world has come here as a student or a teacher, including the Libenskis from Czechoslovakia, Jan Erik Ritzman from Sweden and several Venetians. This year Jim Dine and Judy Pfaff are among the artists-in-residence. The current artistic director, the artist Pike Powers, describes Pilchuck's mission as, "One foot in the experimental, one foot in tradition. We are committed to remaining very open and very intense. We were started with a 'you-can-do-it' attitude and everyone who comes gets ignited by it." The school is a private, not-for-profit organisation which raises most of its income through a benefit auction (last year's sale of ten items raised around $1.3 million) and private donations.

Lino Tagliapietra, the master glassblower whom Chihuly describes as "the best glassblower in Italy, which basically means the world," has come to Pilchuck every summer since 1979, when he replaced his brother-in-law Cecco Ongaro. Thanks to him, the terms "filigrano," "battuto" and "inciso" are standard vocabulary here for the delicate effects kept secret by centuries of Venetian glassblowers. Although it was no longer punishable by death to transmit these techniques, as it was in the Renaissance, glassblowing remained veiled in mystery in Italy well into the twentieth century and consequently was becoming a dying art there. "People sometimes say terrible things because I went to the States," Tagliapietra said in *Pilchuck: A Glass School* (1996), which charts the history of the place. "The reason I left Murano is because Murano did not give me the opportunity to stay there." At Pilchuck Tagliapietra found the students' freedom exhilarating. "The boldness was so new to me. On the one hand it was a shock—the lack of a cultural base, the absence of traditions. But on the other hand it was very inspiring for my own work." Lino opened all of the secrets of Venetian glass and once he arrived at Pilchuck, everyone realised they had been doing it wrong. In the early days, he observed that American glassblowing was like "working with a wood chisel—but holding the knife end in your hand and working with the handle."

"Lino is a force. He loves to cook as much as he loves to teach people about glassblowing," says Chihuly. "Glassblowing is a group effort. It requires a team of between three and fifteen people and to be a great artist, you have to be a real leader. You can't just be good at it; you have to be able to inspire your team."

Tagliapietra now shuttles between Venice and Seattle and his career has taken off in both places, with his one-of-a-kind works selling in the five and six figures. His refined, sculptural pieces are a far cry from Dale's free-form creations, but there is enough room for both at Pilchuck and in today's thriving market for glass. "Lino is more of a master, whereas Dale is more of a ring-leader," says Josiah McElheny, a young glass artist who has worked with them both.

It is this "ring-leader" role that best defines Chihuly. For though he admires fellow artists such as David Hockney (Chihuly recently bought one of Hockney's "Grand Canyon" colour Xeroxes for his desert home and Hockney has two Chihulys on his grand piano), it is Andy Warhol with whom he most identifies. In the early 1980s Chihuly and Warhol traded pieces with each other: Warhol chose a "Sea Form" and Chihuly chose a dollar bill silk screen. Andy had the factory; Dale has the boathouse. Group participation is essential to both of their work, although where Warhol had a darkly ironic side, Chihuly runs on manic enthusiasm. It is as hard to imagine Warhol shouting "Wow! Cool stuff" as it is to imagine Chihuly wearing black.

"Warhol is my favourite artist, and there are still so many sides of him that haven't been completely explored: his movies, magazines, bands," enthuses Chihuly. "What struck me most about meeting him was that he seemed honest. Unlike most artists, if you asked him how long a piece took to make, or how many pieces he had made, he would never lie. Artists, of all people, should tell the truth."

Reprinted with permission from
The Tacoma News Tribune,
September 30, 1999, by Peggy Anderson,
Associated Press Writer

A Melting Wall in Jerusalem

Glass wizard Dale Chihuly, a flamboyant showman whose dazzling, delicate, outsize works have dangled over the canals of Venice and now glitter amid ancient stones in Israel, is building a new wall in Jerusalem's walled Old City.

But this wall—up to 60 feet long and 20 feet tall—will be made of ice, melting in the desert sun as a symbol of how the barriers dividing people in the tense Mideast may someday melt away.

Ice from an artesian well in an Alaska quarry—64 tons of it, in 6- by 5- by 3-foot slabs—is en route to Israel for Sunday's planned installation, which may be the first Chihuly undertaking in decades that does not involve glass or plastic.

"Alaska is about as far away as you can be from Israel," Chihuly mused one recent sunny morning at his Seattle boathouse studio on the shores of Lake Union. But the ice is "unbelievably clear" and perfect for this project. "I've always liked the idea of ice in the desert," said Chihuly, 57, who lived in an Israeli kibbutz in 1962.

Chihuly stopped glassblowing in 1976 when he lost one eye in a car accident. Now he oversees a Renaissance-style studio operation in which dozens of glass artists execute his visions. For this one, they'll be working with ice and light.

Coddled, beneficent and unmistakable with his electric ragdoll hair and black eye patch, he spins his dreams of light and color in a rambling boathouse crammed with workers, friends and family.

For his latest work, he had considered projects in the Negev Desert and the Dead Sea. But he decided on Jerusalem, where a yearlong exhibit at the Tower of David Museum—"Chihuly in the Light of Jerusalem 2000," featuring thousands of pieces of fantastically colored and shaped glass—has drawn 200,000 visitors since July. It seems fitting, he said.

"Jerusalem proper was a walled city—one of the great walled cities of the world," Chihuly said. It had fortifications up to 60 feet high around the citadel that houses the museum. The ice barrier will be outside the citadel near a busy highway, enabling motorists and passers-by to see it free of charge.

It will melt within a week, which could be seen as symbolizing the dissolution of other kinds of barriers. Or "melting tensions. Anything I could do to help melt tensions over there," he said.

"I'd like to think it will make people feel good," Chihuly said. "Jerusalem is still pretty divided, east and west. This happens to be right on the border. It could bring together Jews, Muslims and Christians from different parts of the city."

The wall's form is still undecided, but some portions will probably be collapsed, Chihuly said. The big blocks will be fused together using dry ice.

"Everything changes—color, form," as ice melts, he said. The wall will initially be transparent, but over time "the sun will make it more textured, more milky" as the blocks melt, with "water running between them."

Chihuly's glass exhibit at the museum includes the Blue Tower, a fanciful 46-foot pillar made of hundreds of undulating kelp-like pieces, delicate chandeliers, iridescent and brightly colored spheres and oblongs, and forests of glass spears taller than the artist.

In an e-mail to Chihuly's studio, Israeli singer Noa Asher said that since "the Glass Magician . . . set foot in the holy land, people have been obsessed with color and beauty rather than hatred and war. Now that's an achievement."

Chihuly's art is all about light.

"I work in plastic, glass, ice and neon—all transparent materials that light can go through," he said. When people see these materials, "you're looking at light itself."

His earlier ice installations—dating back to the 1960s at the Rhode Island School of Design—were laced with brilliantly colored neon tubing.

The ice wall will be lit from the outside—by the sun in the daytime and by 4,500-watt airport landing lights at night.

"Shooting color through it" will be as dramatic as neon, Chihuly said—"in some ways more dramatic."

The light will sear through the ice in beams, he said—"No movement. Just—boom!"

Ice sculptors in Alaska call the ice he has chosen "Arctic diamonds," said Team Chihuly member Philip Stewart.

Last month, the ice was loaded into refrigerated trucks by Ice Alaska of Fairbanks and hauled by rail to Anchorage, barged to Tacoma, put on a train to New Jersey and then put aboard a ship for delivery last weekend to the Israeli port of Ashdod, where it was offloaded and trucked to Jerusalem.

Chihuly's studio workers are now at Ashdod to help prepare the ice—cleaning off the sawdust that cushioned it during shipping and shaving the block edges smooth and level for stacking.

News Tribune staff writer Jen Graves contributed to this report.

Reprinted with permission from
The Jerusalem Post,
October 8, 1999, by Naomi Ragen

Melting the Barriers

We live in a very practical world. People are cynical. They act, for the most part, out of self-interest, either hidden or blatantly obvious. We've all come to accept this, and to feel that this is reality, the norms of life. And so, when faced with generosity and selflessness on a grand scale, we can only stand in awe, with tears in our eyes and a feeling of revelation in our hearts.

Life, it turns out, doesn't always have to be lived in the small, mean way that self-interest dictates. Sometimes, it can be stupendously impractical, shocking us with its unexpected and unimagined beauty.

There was a dark time in Israel, not so long ago, when a mentally challenged child was something to be whispered about or shunted off quietly to some institution. Some parents, encouraged by social workers and medical personnel, never even bothered to take such children home from the hospital, abandoning them at birth. "Be practical. Do you really need such a burden?" they were often told. For the past 18 years, Beit Issie Shapiro in Ra'anana has brought all the powers of knowledge and all the forces of love to battle this terrible situation. Founded in 1981 in memory of the wonderful man who spent his life helping such children, Beit Issie Shapiro runs day care programs, clinics, and professional training programs which both nurture these children, and encourage their families and communities to embrace them. This weekend I was lucky enough to be invited to join "Mission for a Lifetime," a group of good-hearted and highly successful Americans who are spending some time here learning about what else can be done to melt away those barriers standing between such children and a good, happy, productive life within their own communities. The group was organized and underwritten by Stephanie and Jules Trump of Williams Island in Florida (who are against any publicity, and don't want their names mentioned, but I can't help it, because I love them. So forgive me, will you?)

Beit Issie Shapiro, whose executive director is Naomi Stuchiner, the late Mr. Shapiro's daughter, is truly a labor of love.

It was fitting, therefore, that on Shabbat afternoon all of us walked over to the Old City to see another labor of love, the transformation of the Tower of David by the spectacular beauty of world-renown glass artist Dale Chihuly's sculptures.

Rising over the stark white Jerusalem stones like bubbles or sea creatures, the shimmering glass in brilliant colors are indescribably wondrous.

But most wondrous of all was the animating spirit of the artist, widely hailed as one of the great glass artists of the 20th century. The installation at the Tower of David cost the artist $500,000 out of his own pocket, over and above the support given by the municipality and the Clore and Jerusalem foundations.

It was worth every penny, he said, to see a quarter of a million people from all over Israel flooding through Jaffa Gate once again, a place most Israelis have avoided since the intifada began. It is his homage to Jerusalem on the eve of the millennium, to bring "pleasure and happiness to people in one of the most historic, exotic and beautiful cities of the world."

The crowning finale of the Chihuly exhibit was the 64 tons of special blue ice shipped from Alaska and sculpted into a symbolic wall where Jewish and Arab Jerusalem meet. Even the guards keeping the public back were rubbing their eyes at the sight. A mirage. Ice in the desert.

Destined to melt in only a few days.

"We want it to melt. It's supposed to melt," Dale Chihuly told us. Barriers between Jew and Arab, divisions, conflicts. Like blue Alaskan ice in the summer sun.

The ice wall evoked all kinds of reactions: There was outright contempt in the words of the municipal worker beside me; a gleam of amusement in the eyes of police guards; shock and excitement rippling through a passing platoon of soldiers, who broke ranks and scurried over to touch the massive cold blocks. And for the rest of us, who just stared at it, mesmerized, an experience of awe, and a strange, secret joy in seeing so lovely and unexpected a thing happening before our eyes.

Bless you, Issie Shapiro, your wife, your kind children and grandchildren; the Trumps, and all the other wonderful people who stand shoulder to shoulder with your vision, helping to melt away all those barriers preventing children with disabilities from showing us who they are, what they can be, with a little help from their friends.

And bless you, Dale Chihuly, for your immense generosity—both spiritual and material—for your humility, and for sharing the madness and spectacular beauty of your unique artistic vision.

Bless you all, for helping the rest of us to see and feel a different kind of reality. For insisting we see not just the cynicism of what is, but the revelation of what can be.

Reprinted with permission from
The Independent, London
October 9, 1999, by Phil Reeves

Wall of Arctic Ice Melts Quicker than Middle East's Tensions

Groups of perplexed people gathered this week outside Jerusalem's Old City to stare at a wall of ice, brought from Alaska. The person behind this creation was the American glass artist, Dale Chihuly. The ice was—said the PR spin—intended to "mirror the Middle East's melting tensions."

The week proved a hot one—both for the ice and for the region's politicians.

On Saturday, 20 men labour through the night unloading 64 tons of ice and assembling it into a wall. It will stand beneath the Old City's western wall, built by Suleiman the Magnificent in 1542. When the Ottoman architects ran into problems, he chopped off their heads. Chihuly's team also encounters hitches: bricks are broken. They scatter them around, to look like ruins.

Three members of Islamic Jihad escape from prison.

It is hot on Sunday. Chihuly's team is running a sweep on how long the ice will take to melt. Chihuly predicts 10 days. Now, with water pouring off the 12ft wall, 48 hours seems more likely. This is disappointing, given that the project cost $250,000 (£156,000).

The opening of an overland passage to allow Palestinians to travel between Gaza and the West Bank is postponed today because of security arguments.

He is odd-looking, Dale Chihuly. A mop of curls crowns a jowly face that looks as if it was, like his works, blown out of glass. On Monday the 58-year-old wears lime coloured jeans, paint-spattered boots and a black patch over one eye.

The patch is a result of a head-on car crash in Britain when he was on his way to Bath to see the artist, Peter Blake. He also knows David Hockney, and is soon to have tea with the Queen. Not bad for a college drop-out. These days he's billed as "one of the century's greatest glass artists," and fêted for once hanging chandeliers over Venice's canals. In 1992, America's state governors anointed him the US's first "national living treasure." Chihuly says his wall was really intended as a present to Jerusalemites, 300,000 of whom have visited the current glass exhibition at the Tower of David Museum. But he also underscores its symbolism as a monument to an improving Middle East. "Let people live side by side. No more bloodshed and grief!" he cries.

Today students on the West Bank burn a model of a Jewish temple as a protest about a Disney exhibit in Florida that refers to Jerusalem as "the heart of the Jewish people." It is still hot on Tuesday and the ice is disappearing fast.

Israeli and Palestinian negotiators have agreed on terms for the West Bank–Gaza passage but no date is set for the opening. The conditions to which traveling Palestinians must comply seem draconian.

By Wednesday, the wall is just a few small cubes of ice.

The Israeli army says it has sealed off the West Bank farmland to replace training zones in areas handed over to the Palestinians...

On Thursday the Palestinians say they will boycott negotiations with Israel about a permanent peace treaty until Israel stops building settlements on occupied land. Israel postpones the release of 151 Palestinian prisoners on Friday in a dispute over who will go free. The ice wall has vanished, but the politics remains. Peace in the Middle East is going to require a slower thaw.

Reprinted with permission from
Hadassah Magazine,
December 1999, by Sharon Kanon

Color with a Touch of Glass

From its earthy origins, glass expands into luminous, transcendent beauty. The world's master glassblower has been infusing his creations with power and strength and sets them out to heal the world—this time amid Jerusalem's eternal stones.

Why would the world's most celebrated glass artist create his largest exhibition—a feat of logistics—in Jerusalem?

It's the millennium, of course.

"We are going full circle," explains Dale Chihuly, the glass impresario who with his red silk shirt and chartreuse jeans, paint-speckled orthopedic shoes and black eyepatch is the image of the bohemian artist. "We are returning to the origins of glass 5,000 years ago."

Preparation included meeting with archeologists and studying the history of the city and ancient glassblowing, which was likely invented by the Phoenicians 2,000 years ago. Early evidence of glass bubbles was uncovered in a first-century B.C.E. workshop in the Old City. It is also believed there were glass windows in the Holy Temple (in Job, glass is equated with gold). Chihuly, who is not Jewish, was struck by the similarity between some of his own work and ancient styles and that some works were made purely for beauty.

Fascinated by the historical connection between the Middle East and glassmaking, Chihuly—until now best known for his mammoth outdoor installations in Venice,

Vianne (France) and the island of Niijima (Japan)—has set his outsized, brilliantly colored, fluid yet delicate sculptures against the background of the starkly rugged and multilevel stones of the Tower of David Museum of the History of Jerusalem, also known as the Citadel.

The exhibition, "Chihuly in the Light of Jerusalem 2000," which opened in July, is drawing record crowds—70,000 the first month. And when it ends in the spring, people will still be able to see his work at the Tower and at the Israel Museum, both of which expect to acquire an installation. (If you don't make it to Israel any time soon, check out the Web site: www.chihuly.com.) But the 58-year-old master, who has been creating large-scale environmental works since 1967 and whose pieces are in the collections of 165 museums, hopes his creations will be more than an esthetic experience.

"Jerusalem is the headquarters of three of the mightiest religions of the world, and our crystals are going to help them forget their differences," says Chihuly, whose home base is the Boathouse, his studio in Seattle, where he employs 120 in his hotshop.

Certainly the works are testimony to the forces of light, beauty, wonderment, good energy and esthetic pleasure. "I liked the social situation," observes Avivah Gottlieb Zornberg, author and teacher of Torah. "The exhibition was daring, beautiful. It created a good feeling. Everyone was filled with happiness."

Not everyone will see the same thing. Depending on their tradition, visitors to the most ambitious work, Crystal Mountain, for instance, say the towering pink installation looks, variously, like the Burning Bush, Mount Sinai, rock candy—even the Crucifixion.

The city, site and panoramic view are part of the draw. Chihuly conceived the project when he was in Jerusalem two and a half years ago for a memorial service for Izzika Gaon, former curator of design at the Israel Museum. Gaon had once suggested that Chihuly install his glassworks in the Tower of David. He says the project "energized" him for the year that he and 60 assistants (half of them in Israel) worked on it.

"I thought Venice was the ultimate city, but the stone and the history of Jerusalem, its complexity, make this an even more fascinating place. It couldn't be more beautiful. The juxtaposition of stone, one of the hardest materials that has stood the test of time, and glass, the most fragile, transparent material, gave me another reason to work in this great city."

The dramatic installations are startling ornaments for a fortress that tells the complex tale of Jerusalem's conquest from the time of the Hasmoneans through the Romans, Byzantines, Mamaluks, Crusaders, Muslims and Ottomans, until the Six-Day War when Israel reunited the city. The mighty walls of the ruins and multiple levels from these different periods challenged Chihuly to do justice to both the Citadel and the installations. Chihuly made his pieces larger than any he had created before. He used more than 10,000 glittering pieces of glass weighing 47 tons and requiring a shipment of a dozen 40-foot containers to create wonders valued at almost $10 million, according to a museum spokesperson.

The show begins after a visitor crosses the Crusader moat; inside the Tower, on video,

Chihuly talks about his work. Right after the entrance, look up and you will see a lovely yellow "chandelier" hanging high in the dome of the hexagonal Mamaluk tower. With outward curving, interlocking arms, the cylindrical piece beams from light that enters from the outside. Go outdoors and above you is the nature-defying Moon, made of blue and white glass spheres on a metal frame, strapped to the tower's dome. The Moon and Crystal Mountain are visible outside the museum.

Looking down from the ramparts, below the ruins of King Herod's magnificent palace are large multicolored spheres—gold, speckled and streaked. They represent the artist's embellished version of Japanese Fishing Floats used to hold fishing nets.

Although they look simple, Chihuly says "[the floats] are physically the most difficult single forms we have ever done . . . when you get up to this scale, as much as 40 inches in diameter." A collector of authentic Japanese floats—who can remember them washing up on the shores of the Pacific Northwest when he was a child in Tacoma, Washington—Chihuly placed his own Niijima floats in the Byzantine cistern.

Also on display are 200 vase-shaped and high-necked pieces made from blue glass used in the 500-year-old Hebron Glass Factory, where Chihuly worked (he also used facilities in Finland, France, Japan, the United States and the Czech Republic for this project).

Charming in simplicity, small black herons perch atop the Herodian ruins, and the sleek Black Saguaro cacti, narrow with bulbous tops, planted on the rocky Hasmonean wall, command attention. On an adjacent ledge

sprout green blades of glass, bright as an emerging Garden of Eden.

The three installations most likely to catch your eye as you enter the courtyard are the Blue Tower, Red Spears and Crystal Mountain. The first is comprised of 2,000 glass tendrils (each anchored with steel armature) in shades from pale sapphire at its base to deep cobalt blue at the top; the triangular-shaped structure rises 48 feet from the original ground level of the Hasmonean fortress. Red Spears, a conical structure of stacked, luminous rods, emerges from the twelfth-century Crusader remains in the courtyard. (There are also Yellow Spears planted vertically in the courtyard.)

The 48-foot Crystal Mountain, weighing over 60 tons, is supported by five miles of steel rods and 18,000 welds. "It would have weighed four times more if we had used glass," asserts Philip Stewart, a technician whose challenge was to make the structure look gossamer despite the steel. It is made from polyvitro, plastic cast in molds made from chunks of glass.

Crystal Mountain also has a musical dimension. Listen carefully and you will hear sounds—a subtle tingle intermingled with the sound of church bells, a Gregorian chant, a muezzin calling Muslims to prayer, a cello with a cantorial sound, a cantor praying. "Jerusalem resonates with prayer every day," says Jonathan Berger, associate professor of music at Stanford University's Center for Computer Research in Music and Acoustics, who synthesized the religious sounds of the Old City and programmed them to play at the appropriate prayer times. Special music is heard on holidays. The composer was commissioned by Chihuly and the Tower of

David Museum to sculpt sound interacting with the environment.

The effect of "Echoes of Light and Time" was achieved by placing eight sensors among the crystals to pick up the changing intensity of light and heat, the movement of the sun through the glass.

"The sculpture is like a sonic sundial that hears the shadow and regulates the intensity of the recorded music," Berger explains. "Clouds, birds flying overhead, changing seasons, ever-changing light create infinite possibilities. Every time the prayer will sound slightly different."

Not all the works are huge. At the entrance to the Crusader Hall are the Jerusalem Cylinders, six handsome vase-like pieces with chunks of crystal affixed asymmetrically. Seaforms—spiraling, delicate and breathtaking coral-like shells—express their creator's love for the sea; Chihuly once worked as a commercial fisherman. "Blowing the pieces into ribbed steel molds gives them strength, like corrugated cardboard," he explains. Probably his most prolific series are those on the Persian Ceiling. Named for their rich color, they are like giant butterflies or jellyfish that can be mounted on walls. The seaworld often comes in sets like the gorgeous fusion of circular and ribbed shapes in tangerine-coral, green, brown and gold hues. Chihuly's paintings of the installations are also on display; they sell from $3,000 to $5,000; the large installations go from $25,000 to $1 million. Besides British royalty and major museums, Chihuly's works have been purchased by the Clintons, the Kennedys, Elton John, Robin Williams and "virtually every millionaire in the Northwest," he says.

An inveterate traveler, Chihuly says his three weeks in Israel have been the longest he's stayed in one place for a long time. But 36 years ago he spent a year on Kibbutz Lahav in the Negev.

"It was a life-changing experience," here calls thoughtfully. "I went from being a boy to being a man." Several people influenced him, "especially a young man my own age who had a cause, a purpose in life. I went back home and decided it was time to get serious." The glass may best be appreciated at night. "It was so beautiful, especially when you see the play of light in the evening," said Estelle Fink, curator of the Museum of Jewish Art at Heichal Shlomo. "[The glassworks] belong in the Tower; they're one of the seven wonders."

Danny Kalderon, head of glassworks at Bezalel Academy and himself a glass artist, was pleased that there was an opportunity for people to see large-scale glass art. "It was wonderful to see such large works, with so many colors—studio glass, not made in a factory." He recommends seeing the exhibition at sunset because "it reflects more, like a jewel."

As an additional gesture, in October the artist constructed outside the Jaffa Gate an illuminated Jerusalem Wall of Ice from 24 blocks of Alaskan ice. The 64 tons, which melted in two days (and cost Chihuly and Boeing, a Seattle company, $300,000), symbolized the melting of tension between the Israelis and Palestinians.

"Up until the Six-Day War, the [Tower] was a fortress," Chihuly notes. "It gives me great pleasure to open it up as a place to enjoy art and give the message of hope and peace. Glass has a healing quality."

Reprinted with permission from
Scientific American Discovering Archaeology,
January/February 2000, by Lisa Parks

Israel's Fragile Legacy: 2000 Years of Glassblowing

Along with Israel's spectacular archaeological legacy is another vividly colorful heritage: the timeless art of shaping glass. About 2,000 years ago, artisans in the eastern Mediterranean learned to blow graceful shapes into molten glass.

And a new industry was born.

This year, the Tower of David Museum in Old City, Jerusalem, is tipping its hat to the region's historical contribution to the glass industry with the colorful, yearlong exhibit *Chihuly in the Light of Jerusalem 2000* by world-class American glassmaker Dale Chihuly, who is renowned for such huge glass sculptures as his 1996 installations over the canals of Venice. The Tower of David Museum says the exhibit "will form a central part of Jerusalem's celebrations of the millennium."

Paying homage to the transformation of glass from a medium for decorative vessels to a sculptural material with "endless possibility," Dale Chihuly spins glass into fantasy and history in the courtyard of the museum. The 15 sculptures on display required more than 4,000 pieces of glass and include the 30-foot Crystal Mountain, 44-foot Blue Tower, and an 11-foot blue globe that dangles above the Tower.

Although the art of glassblowing developed in the Syrian/Israeli region, glassmaking itself appeared thousands of years earlier. We will probably never know the source of glass-making, but an early story by the Roman historian Pliny the Elder (A.D. 23–79) credits Phoenician sailors with accidentally discovering the process. While trying to start a fire to cook dinner, they apparently propped a cooking pot on blocks of soda (sodium carbonate) from the ship's cargo. The crew was flabbergasted to find (on the sand under their dinner pot) a stream of liquid that later hardened into glass.

Glassy fragments may have first appeared as unvalued byproducts of smelting copper, firing ceramics, or heating pots on sandy soils. Although thousands of different chemical compositions can be made into glass, the most common early mixture was a silicate material (especially sand) heated with soda, which lowers the sand's melting point, and lime to stabilize the glass. Glass also occurs naturally in the form of obsidian (a volcanic material), tektite (from meteor impacts), and fulgurite (a cylindrical glass that forms when lightning strikes sand).

Glassmaking was likely a giant, trial-and-error experiment conducted over centuries. The first true glass artifacts were beads, which surfaced in Mesopotamia over 5,000 years ago. From there, progress limped along until the appearance, 1,000 years later, of hollowed-glass forms which were produced by core forming. In this early production method, molten glass was trailed around a core supported by a rod to form a vessel. The object was removed and cooled, then the inside was scraped out.

The Egyptians may have learned from the Syrians how to produce faience beads and bottles. But Syria and Mesopotamia remained the glassy heart of the new craft. Until about 50 B.C., glassmaking was a labor of patience. The time-intensive techniques of core forming, casting (forming glass in a mold), and cutting (removing glass from an object's surface by grinding) required days for a single bottle. Glass, a luxury item as precious and rare as gold, became the province of the rich.

But the invention of glassblowing blew the roof off the exclusivity of glass. For the first time, glass could be mass-produced, making it inexpensive and available to everyone. One person's labor could yield dozens of objects a day—instead of a single object produced over several days.

The process was developed in the first century B.C. on the Syro-Palestinian coast, where artisans learned to gather molten glass on the end of a hollow pipe, then blow through it to inflate the viscous mass like a bubble. It could be freely shaped with simple tools, or blown into a hollow mold to give it a desired form.

A 1950s construction project at a cave in the Galilee area of Israel turned up a remnant of the ancient glassmaking tradition. Located next to the Jewish cemetery of Beth She'arim, the cave contained a nine-ton chunk of manufactured glass. Made some 1,600 years ago, its size is surpassed only by the giant telescope mirrors of the twentieth century. The raw glass was meant to be dispersed among smaller factories, where artisans could soften and rework it. Instead, for unknown reasons, the slab was abandoned. When the Roman Empire fanned out in the first century B.C. to embrace the eastern Mediterranean, its trade networks encompassed the glass centers of Syria-Palestine (modern Syria and Israel) and Egypt, and glassblowing techniques spread over a vast

area. Emperor Augustus (27 B.C. to A.D. 14) is credited as the impetus for mass production of glass. In an effort to concentrate crafts on the Italian mainland, he imported Syrian and Judean glass craftsmen as slaves. Within a decade, the easily acquired glass became as popular as pottery for storage of everything from fish to perfume.

The glassmaking profession was valued to the point of secrecy in ancient history. A 3,300-year-old cuneiform tablet from Mesopotamia gives clandestine instructions, recopied over the centuries, for furnace-building and glassmaking. Artisans were directed to allow no stranger on the premises and, on the day of glassmaking, to perform libations, pray, and sacrifice a sheep in front of sacred images hung on the furnace. Pliny the Elder, describing the glass of Rome, enthusiastically writes in his volume *Natural History*, "We have done things that will be deemed mythical by those who come after us." On the Venetian glassmaking island of Murano—at its zenith from A.D. 1400–1700—glassmakers were forbidden to leave Venice on penalty of death, in order to guard the secret of Venetian glass.

Nevertheless, some managed to sneak away and set up factories in other European cities. Stained glass, lacquer glass, uranium glass, studio glass, milk glass, peachblow glass, carnival glass—the glass industry has sprouted in many directions through the centuries. Surprisingly, however, glassblowers had developed almost all the major decorative techniques that are used by glass artists today within a few hundred years of the invention of free-blowing.

The profession has produced such talents as Louis Comfort Tiffany, Rene Lalique, and

Frank Fenton. But not until the studio-glass movement, of which Dale Chihuly is a part, did glass become a valued sculptural medium. The exhibit at the Tower of David Museum, which was created by Chihuly and 80 workers, recognizes the origins and development of the glass craft. The exhibit remains open until June 30, 2000.

Chihuly, who worked on an Israeli kibbutz in the early 1960s, wanted to stage an exhibition in Jerusalem because, for him, it is "one of the most historic, exotic, and beautiful cities in the world. It is second to none in its richness and texture."

Reprinted with permission from
The Miami Herald, February 2, 2000,
by Larry Kaplow (Cox News Service)

Israelis Revisit Old Jerusalem

JERUSALEM—These days, Israeli Yael Boksenboin can visit Jerusalem's Old City like a tourist—with her toddler daughter and without the rifle she used to carry.

She was a soldier in the Old City during the Palestinian intifada uprising that swept the region 10 years ago. Then, this tourist haven—an ancient walled district in downtown Jerusalem—was the scene of frequent Palestinian attacks on Jews.

There was a permanent Israeli presence in the small Jewish Quarter. But most Israelis halted what had been frequent shopping or dining excursions to the Old City.

When the intifada ended in 1993, the fear remained. So did Israeli troops, stationed along the narrow streets.

But, in the last year, Israelis have been rediscovering the Old City. Especially on Saturdays, Hebrew can be heard sprinkled among the Spanish, English and Italian of the foreign sightseers and the Arabic of the locals.

When Boksenboin, a 30-year-old lawyer, visited a couple of months ago, it was the first time in 10 years.

She strolled by the Western Wall, sacred to Jews. She took in the scents of the bazaar's spices and humus, which she recalled from her visits as a child.

"The last time I was here I was a soldier and I walked with a gun," she said. "I don't have to look behind my back like I used to. It feels good."

Exactly why Israelis are returning now is not clear. People cite the current rarity of political violence. Some say that progress in the peace process makes them feel more at ease among Arabs.

Whatever the reason, Israelis are feeling more at home in the heart of their cherished, yet disputed, capital.

"It's a very good sign," says Israeli Meron Benvenisti, who was a top city official during the intifada and saw the decline in Israeli visits to the Old City.

"They used to define the whole thing as the geography of fear. People are overcoming the fear," said Benvenisti, whose book City of Stone describes the city's ethnic tensions.

It is still rare for Israelis to venture into other Arab areas of Jerusalem. Benvenisti is skeptical that the political climate is responsible for their return to the Old City. He said the lack of recent violence has prompted Israelis to simply rediscover a delight they had missed.

"It's really a phenomenon," said Israeli tour guide Doron Bar, who was leading a group of Israelis recently.

Much of the credit may belong to an exhibit of works from American glass sculptor Dale Chihuly. Opened in July in a museum garden just inside the Old City walls, it has sold nearly 700,000 tickets to foreigners and Israelis.

From the exhibit, many venture farther to Old City shops and restaurants.

The Old City is less than a square mile in area and dates back more than 3,000 years. Its stone streets are lined by more than 3,000 shops, selling everything from tacky tourist T-shirts to the meat, vegetables and clothes used by the locals. They also offer fine jewelry, pottery and carpets from throughout the Middle East.

Israel took total control over the Old City when it captured it from the Jordanians in 1967. Palestinians seek to govern their own affairs there; most other countries officially consider the matter up for negotiation.

The Palestinian merchants seem pleased to see Israeli shoppers returning.

Recently, Palestinian Adel Kawasmi has seen the return of a few Israelis who came to his shop regularly before the intifada to share tea and buy his glass bowls and drinking glasses.

"We are happy to see them here, of course," he said. "The business is much better."

Fax Transcription

Page 16

Dear Mighty,

So let me tell you more about all the glass that we are shipping to the Citadel as we speak. Ten 40' containers, Mighty, coming from the USA, France, Finland, Czech Republic, and Japan, about 10,000 pieces in all! Since before you were conceived in Venice, Mighty, I've been going back and forth to Jerusalem thinking about this extraordinary Citadel—marveling at its beauty and strength and texture and color—its history, its sense of place, its meaning to us all. Every time I visited the Citadel I would imagine what I could do to enhance its glory and bring attention to its soul.

Page 17

Mighty- wait 'til you see the Crystal Mountain.

Page 18

Mighty, We'll have to get mountain climbers from Israel or elsewhere to scale the Citadel walls both outside and inside to put flowers—thousands of them—coming out of everywhere. Imagine, Mighty, with the sun coming through them!

Page 19

Moon Ball is the name of this one, Mighty. Sorry about my writing—it's bumpy on this Tokyo–San Francisco run on April 26, 1999. I just went to my show in Hiroshima, another city like Jerusalem that had to be rebuilt many times from the scars of war. The Moon Ball is going to be blue/green colors, something like the Atlantis piece.

Page 20

Yellow Fish: they've been called. These too were made in France. There's only about 25 of them and they're in a beautiful uranium yellow color. Hope you don't get bored with all this glass, Mighty, but there'll be all kinds of Team members that will want to play with you, and lots of visitors and friends that are coming.

Page 21

Mighty, the glassblowers like to name the forms sometimes while they are blowing them. They call these the Blue Herons. There'll be a couple hundred of these Herons—maybe coming out of one of the Towers. Some of them are black.

Page 22

Black and Red Saguaros—they look a little like those big cacti from Sonoran Desert in Arizona, Mighty, and they'll feel right at home in the nearby Desert of Israel. We'll put them on top of one of the towers. I think we have a couple of hundred of them. They were made in Finland.

Page 23

The tallest piece in Jerusalem, Mighty, will be the Feather Blue Tower, at about 70' high! Wow, that's really high for us, Mighty. You'll be able to see it real good from inside and outside of the Citadel. It'll have over 2000 parts, Mighty. You'll want to watch this one being erected—me too.

Page 24

Mighty, I made about 20 white Belugas a couple of years ago in Vianne, France. I kept the Belugas along with a lot of other forms we made in France and sent them all to Jerusalem. I think I'll install the Belugas in the grassy part of the Citadel. We'll see.

Page 25

Mighty, I call these Spears, and they can be as long as 20 feet—the longest forms I've ever blown. I usually like them in red and orange, but not always. We'll have about 500 Spears in Jerusalem.

Page 26
Moon Ball

Page 27
Floats in the ancient village
    Chihuly
    37,000' en route Tokyo
    4·22·99

The people
who made it possible

Marianne and Doron Livnat
Robert Weil
Department of Culture, Jerusalem Municipality
Economic Company of Jerusalem, Ltd.
New Pan, representatives of Toshiba and Kenwood in Israel
Avi Cranes
Boeing Corporation

The Jerusalem Foundation,
thanks to generous gifts from
Leonard Dobbs,
Vivian Clore-Duffield through The Clore Foundation,
The Charles and Lynn Schusterman Foundation,
The J. Ira and Nicki Harris Foundation,
and an anonymous friend from the US.

What a Team!
Israel / American
Thank You Everybody

love Chihuly

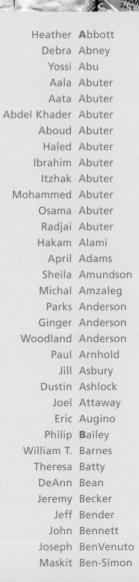

Heather **A**bbott
Debra Abney
Yossi Abu
Aala Abuter
Aata Abuter
Abdel Khader Abuter
Aboud Abuter
Haled Abuter
Ibrahim Abuter
Itzhak Abuter
Mohammed Abuter
Osama Abuter
Radjai Abuter
Hakam Alami
April Adams
Sheila Amundson
Michal Amzaleg
Parks Anderson
Ginger Anderson
Woodland Anderson
Paul Arnhold
Jill Asbury
Dustin Ashlock
Joel Attaway
Eric Augino
Philip **B**ailey
William T. Barnes
Theresa Batty
DeAnn Bean
Jeremy Becker
Jeff Bender
John Bennett
Joseph BenVenuto
Maskit Ben-Simon

and

Advertising	Vieder Sigawi, Ltd.
Crane Work	Avi Crane
Israeli Glass	Hebron Glass and Ceramics Factory
Lighting	Uri Gabai - Light and Communications Ltd.
Metal Work	Zion Nachmani Welders
Platform Construction	Sherutei Bama Plus Ltd.
Transportation	InterDel
	Yair Pines

טדי קולק
تيدي كوليك
Teddy Kollek

January 10, 2000

Mr. Dale Chihuly
Chihuly Inc.
111 NW 50th Street
Seattle, Washington 98107-5120

Dear friend Chihuly:

I am encouraged to write to you every time that I pass by the Tower of David and see
the multitudes still coming to your exhibition. There have been 600,000 visitors so
far and they are still coming.

You cannot imagine how much you have done for Jerusalem. Many people are
coming to the city just to see your exhibition. People that in the past have been afraid
to visit Jerusalem and the Old City are now seeing the city in a new light. No
politician could have achieved this and we are very grateful to you for making this
possible. I wanted to write with my personal thank you.

With warm regards and every good wish for a hopeful new Millennium.

and in gratitude   Yours, *ever*

Teddy

Teddy Kollek

11 Rivka Street POB 10185
Jerusalem Israel, 91101
Tel: 972-2-6751703/4
Fax: 972-2-6722385

شارع ريفكه ١١ ص.ب.١٠١٨٥
أورشليم القدس ٩١١٠١
تلفون ٤/٦٧٥١٧٠٣–٢.
فكسيميليا ٦٧٢٢٣٨٥–٢.

רח' רבקה 11 ת"ד 10185
ירושלים 91101
טל: 02-6751703/4
פקס: 02-6722385

E-Mail: teddy@netmedia.net.il : דאר אלקטרוני.

Chronology

1941 Born September 20 in Tacoma, Washington, to George Chihuly and Viola Magnuson Chihuly.

1957 Older brother and only sibling, George, is killed in a Navy Air Force training accident in Pensacola, Florida.

1958 His father suffers a fatal heart attack at age fifty-one. His mother goes to work to support herself and Dale.

1959 Graduates from high school in Tacoma and enrolls in the College of Puget Sound (now the University of Puget Sound). Transfers to the University of Washington in Seattle to study interior design and architecture.

1962 Travels to Florence to study art. Goes to Paris and the Middle East for the first time.

1963 Works on a kibbutz in the Negev Desert. Meets architect Robert Landsman. Redirected after meeting Landsman, he returns to the University of Washington and studies under Hope Foote and Warren Hill.

1964 While still a student, receives the Seattle Weavers Guild Award for his innovative use of glass and fiber.

1965 Receives B.A. in Interior Design from the University of Washington. Textile designer Jack Lenor Larsen becomes a mentor and friend. Experimenting on his own, Chihuly blows his first glass bubble, using colored flat glass and metal pipe.

1966 Enters the University of Wisconsin at Madison on a full scholarship to study glass under Harvey Littleton.

1967 Receives M.S. in Sculpture from the University of Wisconsin. Enrolls at the Rhode Island School of Design (RISD) in Providence, where he begins his exploration of environmental works using neon, argon, and blown glass. Italo Scanga lectures at RISD, and the two begin a lifelong friendship. They consider themselves brothers.

1968 Receives M.F.A. in Ceramics from RISD. Awarded a Louis Comfort Tiffany Foundation Grant and a Fulbright Fellowship, enabling him to travel and work in Europe. Becomes the first American glassblower to work in the prestigious Venini Fabrica on the island of Murano. Returns to the United States and spends the summer teaching at Haystack Mountain School of Crafts in Deer Isle, Maine.

1969 Meets glass masters Erwin Eisch in Germany and Jaroslava Brychtová and Stanislav Libenský in Czechoslovakia. Returning to the United States, Chihuly joins RISD faculty as an Instructor in Ceramics. Establishes the glass program at RISD.

1971 The Pilchuck Glass School is founded with the support of Anne Gould Hauberg and John Hauberg. Works with John Landon and James Carpenter to develop Pilchuck, which will have a profound impact on artists working in glass worldwide. He resumes teaching at RISD and creates pivotal works *20,000 Pounds of Ice and Neon* and *Glass Forest #1* and *#2* with Carpenter.

1974 Tours European glass centers with Thomas Buechner of the Corning Museum of Glass and Paul Schulze of Steuben Glass. Upon returning to the United States, he builds a glass shop for the Institute of American Indian Arts in Santa Fe, New Mexico.

1975 At RISD, begins *Navajo Blanket Cylinders*. Kate Elliott and later Flora Mace fabricate the complex thread drawings. Begins *Irish* and *Ulysses Cylinders* with Seaver Leslie; Mace executes the glass drawings.

1976 An automobile accident in England leaves him without sight in his left eye and with permanent damage to his right ankle and foot. Returns to Providence to serve as Head of the Department of Sculpture and the Program in Glass at RISD.

1977 Inspired by Northwest Coast Indian baskets, he begins the *Basket* series at Pilchuck over the summer.

1978 Meets William Morris, and they begin a close, eight-year working relationship. A solo show, *Baskets and Cylinders: Recent Glass by Dale Chihuly*, is curated by Michael W. Monroe at the Renwick Gallery of the National Museum of American Art, Smithsonian Institution, Washington, D.C.

1979 Dislocates his shoulder and must relinquish the gaffer position for good. Morris becomes his chief gaffer. Chihuly begins to make drawings as a way to communicate his designs.

1980 Resigns as Head of the Program in Glass at RISD. Returns there periodically during the 1980s as artist-in-residence. Begins *Seaform* series at Pilchuck.

1981 Begins *Macchia* series, using up to three hundred colors of glass.

1982 First major book, *Chihuly Glass*, designed by RISD colleague and friend Malcolm Grear, is published.

1983 Returns to the Pacific Northwest after sixteen years on the East Coast.

1984 Begins work on *Soft Cylinder* series, with Flora Mace and Joey Kirkpatrick executing the glass drawings.

1985 Creates several site-specific installations, including *Pink and Gold Braun Seaforms* for the Stouffer Madison Hotel and *Puget Sound Forms* for the Seattle Aquarium. Experiments with *Flower Forms*.

1986 Begins *Persian* series, with Martin Blank as gaffer. With the opening of *Objets de Verre* at the Musée des Arts Décoratifs, Palais du Louvre, in Paris, he becomes one of only four American artists to have had a one-person exhibition at the Louvre. *Chihuly: Color, Glass and Form* published by Kodansha, Tokyo.

1987 Establishes his first hotshop. Donates permanent retrospective collection to the Tacoma Art Museum in honor of his brother and father. Begins association with artist Parks Anderson, commencing with the *Rainbow Room Frieze* at Rockefeller Center in New York City.

1988 Begins *Venetian* series. Working from Chihuly's drawings, Lino Tagliapietra serves as gaffer.

1989 With Italian glass masters Tagliapietra, Pino Signoretto, and a team of glassblowers at Pilchuck, begins *Putti Venetian* series. Working with Tagliapietra, Chihuly creates *Ikebana* series. *Venetians: Dale Chihuly* is published by Twin Palms Publishers.

1990 Purchases the historic Pocock Building on Lake Union, realizing his dream of being on the water in Seattle. Renovates the building and names it The Boathouse for use as a studio, hotshop, archives, and residence. Travels to Japan.

1991 Begins *Niijima Float* series, with Rich Royal as gaffer. Completes large-scale architectural installations, including ones for the GTE World Headquarters and the Yasui Konpira-gu Shinto Shrine in Kyoto, Japan.

1992 Begins *Chandelier* series with large-scale hanging sculpture for the exhibition *Dale Chihuly: Installations 1964–1992*, curated by Patterson Sims at the Seattle Art Museum. Honored as the first National Living Treasure by the Institute for Human Potential, University of North Carolina, Wilmington.

1993 Designs sets for Seattle Opera production of Debussy's *Pelléas et Mélisande*. The *Pilchuck Stumps* are created during this project. Begins *Piccolo Venetian* series with Tagliapietra. Creates *100,000 Pounds of Ice and Neon* as a temporary installation in the Tacoma Dome. *Chihuly Form from Fire* and *Chihuly alla Macchia* are published.

1994 *Chihuly at Union Station*, five large-scale installations for Tacoma's Union Station, a Federal Courthouse, is sponsored by the Executive Council for a Greater Tacoma and organized by the Tacoma Art Museum. Hilltop Artists in Residence, a glassblowing program for at-risk youths in Tacoma, Washington, is created by friend Kathy Kaperick; Chihuly assists with instruction of youths and is a major contributor. Portland Press publishes *Chihuly Baskets* and inaugurates a series of annual Chihuly Studio Editions. Receives the Golden Plate Award from the American Academy of Achievement.

1995 *Cerulean Blue Macchia with Chartreuse Lip Wrap* is added to the White House Collection of American Crafts. Work begins on a project to develop the Museum of Glass in Tacoma and to design and construct the Chihuly Bridge of Glass. *Chihuly Over Venice* begins with a glassblowing session in June in Nuutajärvi, Finland, and a subsequent blow at the Waterford Crystal factory. Creates *Chihuly e Spoleto* installation for the 38th Spoleto Festival of the Two Worlds, in Spoleto, Italy. *Chihuly Seaforms* is published by Portland Press.

1996 Creates a major installation for the Academy of Motion Picture Arts and Sciences Governor's Ball following the Academy Awards ceremony in Hollywood, California. *Chihuly Over Venice* continues with a blow in Monterrey, Mexico. Installs *Chihuly Over Venice*, fourteen *Chandeliers* created and exhibited at various prestigious sites in that city. *Chihuly Over Venice* begins its national tour at the Kemper Museum of Contemporary Art, Kansas City, Missouri. Purchases the Ballard Building in Seattle for use as mock-up and studio space. Creates his first permanent outdoor installation, *Icicle Creek Chandelier*. Portland Press publishes *Chihuly Over Venice* and *Chihuly Persians*.

1997 In his newly renovated Ballard Building, builds a research lab for working with plastics and begins the *Polymar Project*. *Chihuly* is published by Harry N. Abrams, New York. A permanent installation of Chihuly's work opens at the Hakone Glass Forest, Ukai Museum, in Hakone, Japan. The largest-ever Chihuly exhibition, *Chihuly Over Venice* in combination with *Chihuly: The George R. Stroemple Collection*, opens at the Portland Art Museum in Oregon.

1998 A son, Jackson Viola Chihuly, is born February 12 to Dale Chihuly and Leslie Jackson. *Dale Chihuly Icicles: The Icicle Creek Chandelier* is published by Portland Press. Hilltop Artists in Residence program expands to Taos, New Mexico, to work with the Taos Pueblo. Two large Chandeliers are created for Benaroya Hall, the Seattle Symphony's new home. Chihuly's largest sculpture to date, the *Fiori di Como*, is commissioned for the lobby of the Bellagio Resort in Las Vegas. Creates four permanent installations—*Temple of the Sun, Temple of the Moon, Crystal Gate, Atlantis Chandelier*—for the Atlantis Resort on Paradise Island, Bahamas.

1999 Begins *Jerusalem Cylinder* series.

Portland Press publishes *Chihuly Atlantis*, *Chihuly Bellagio*, and *Chihuly Taos Pueblo*. In celebration of the millennium, Chihuly mounts his most ambitious exhibition to date: *Chihuly in the Light of Jerusalem 2000*, for which he creates seventeen installations at the Tower of David Museum of the History of Jerusalem. Travels to the Victoria and Albert Museum, London, to unveil an eighteen-foot *Chandelier* gracing the main entrance of the museum. Returns to Jerusalem in October to create a sixty-foot wall from twenty-four massive blocks of ice.
2000 Designs installations for both the White House Millennium Celebration and Chicago's International Millennium Dinner. Harry N. Abrams publishes *Chihuly Projects*.

This first edition of

Chihuly Jerusalem 2000

is limited to 15,000 casebound copies.
The entire contents are
copyright © Dale Chihuly 2000.
All rights reserved.

Photographs taken by
Parks Anderson
Theresa Batty
Baruch Gian
Donna Goetsch
Itamar Grinberg
Scott Mitchell Leen
Teresa Rishel
Terry Rishel
Zeev Segal
Yehuda Vacknin
William Warmus

Designed by
Anna Katherine Curfman
Laurence Madrelle
Marie Pellaton

with the typefaces
Frutiger and Sabon

on paper
NPI 157 gsm matt art

Printed and bound by
Palace Press International, Hong Kong

Portland Press
P.O. Box 45010
Seattle, Washington 98145
800.574.7272
www.portlandpress.net

ISBN 1-57684-014-X

Mighty

CHIHULY STUDIO 509 NE NORT

TEL 206 632 8707